Croydon
In the 1940s and 1950s

Including many contemporary illustrations from the Croydon Advertiser

Front Cover

North End in 1945, with flags flying from Allders to celebrate VJ (Victory over Japan) Day on 15th August, a few days earlier. Colour photography in the UK was uncertain, expensive and not common before the mid 1950s. Harold Bennett, a professional photographer who lives in Sanderstead, was at the time an RAF pilot with Transport Command and had returned from Canada with some colour film that was far superior to anything obtainable here. He took this splendid shot in the early afternoon on his way to Wilson's Café for tea.

Note that the bus has several windows boarded-up and the tram still bears white paint on its fender from black-out days; these had ended before the cessation of hostilities and by mid 1945 most of the fenders had been repainted.

The Whitgift Hospital (right) shows some evidence of bomb damage.

Frontispiece

The Home Defence procession was held on Saturday 6th May 1939. It was intended to attract more volunteers to take part in training for the country's defence. Starting in Barclay Road, it was led by kilted pipers and drummers from the Brigade of Guards, followed by detachments of the Coldstream and Grenadier Guards, Police, Auxiliary Fire Brigade, Auxiliary Air Force, Air Cadet Corps, St John Ambulance Brigade, Territorial Army and Civil Defence Units interspersed with bands.

The procession went from Barclay Road to Duppas Hill, along Epsom Road and Waddon New Road to the top of Tamworth Road, where it is here seen turning left into London Road. It continued via Broad Green, St James's Road, Wellesley Road, Poplar Walk and North End to Katharine Street where speeches were made by the Mayor, Councillor Edward Stuart Baker, and the Mayoress. Other speeches had been made at various points on the way.

Back Cover

This poster for a Horse Show at Wandle Park in 1948 is a reminder that Croydon was then considered very much a Surrey town as many people regard it still. It also illustrates that the horse continued in use for everyday purposes (see also pages 52 and 53).

Contents

Editor John B. Gent M.C.I.T.

Published by the Croydon Natural History and Scientific Society
96a Brighton Road
South Croydon
Surrey CR2 6AD

ISBN 0 906047 15 3

Printed by DAP (Sussex) Ltd

64 pages   131 illustrations

CROYDON – First Edition – October 1994
Second Edition – October 2000

Price £6.75

1 Evacuation – Monday 4th September 1939

In January 1939 Croydon was declared a Neutral Zone (where evacuation would be unnecessary) under the national Air Raid Precautions Scheme. The Corporation protested and eventually the town was designated an evacuation zone, and plans were prepared.

At 5.30 pm on Saturday 2nd September instructions were received from London that transport and billets would be available within 36 hours. Some 18,000 people were evacuated including teachers, helpers and children under five years old with their mothers. All schoolchildren were labelled and carried gas masks. Many of the local evacuees went to Brighton and Hove.

Here crowds of evacuees are crossing George Street on their way into East Croydon station. The bridge was widened in the 1960s.

2 Gas Masks

By 26th September 1938 over 115,000 Croydonians had received gas masks, and one week after the distribution of this leaflet nearly everyone in the town had been fitted. In the event, gas was never used in attacks on the United Kingdom, but for several years most people carried their masks whenever they left home and practices using tear gas took place from time to time.

Introduction

In 1970 the Croydon Natural History and Scientific Society celebrated its centenary by publishing *Croydon, the Story of a Hundred Years*. Further illustrated books have followed and this one appears as the Society prepares to celebrate its 125th Anniversary in 1995. It is the fourth in a series which provides a visual record of Croydon at different times: *Victorian Croydon Illustrated* covers the 1830s to 1901; *Edwardian Croydon Illustrated* covers 1901 to 1919; and *Croydon Between the Wars* deals with 1919 to 1939. This volume is not a detailed history, but is intended to give a general impression of the town and events between 1939 and 1959, and to encourage those sufficiently interested to carry out further study and research on specific subjects.

Where reference is made to pre-decimal currency, the following conversion table should be used:

Pre-Decimal	Decimal
1d (penny)	just under ½p
6d	2½p
1s 0d (shilling)	5p
2s 6d (half-crown)	12½p

Comparison of wages and prices is always difficult and complicated as living standards and expectations change. The cost of living rose by little more than one third during the war — mostly achieved by strict controls, rationing and some subsidy. In general, manual workers gained

greater increases in wages than others. More general inflation between 1945 and 1955 saw retail prices increase by some 60% and this process continued throughout the 1950s.

In 1939 Croydon was a county borough with a population estimated at 243,400. It was known the world over as the airport for London. The famous bell foundry of Messrs Gillett and Johnston at Whitehorse Road sent its products across the world and there were numerous factories in Purley Way and scattered around the town, which made a wide variety of goods and provided local employment. The well-known stores of Allders, Kennards and Grants attracted shoppers from some distance around.

The adjacent urban district of Coulsdon and Purley (later to be merged with Croydon in 1964 to form the London Borough) had a population estimated at 61,710. Housing development had continued in both areas through the 1930s, mainly to the south and east of the town, but there was still farmland at Addington, Shirley, South Croydon and Coulsdon. The horse was used quite extensively on the farm and for commercial purposes; most milkmen, bakers, greengrocers and coalmen commonly made home deliveries with horse-drawn vehicles. Mechanisation was spreading rapidly but was halted by the war. Few people had cars and frequent bus, tram and trolleybus routes served the town.

The possibility of war had become apparent in the mid-1930s and Croydon Council set up an Air Raid Precautions Committee in 1935. Air Raid Wardens were appointed; recruiting started for fire-fighting, medical and decontamination units. Air Raid Report Centres were established in 1938, and in 1939 there was frantic activity in the building of shelters.

The pages of the *Croydon Advertiser* for 25th August 1939 give a fascinating view of local concerns a week before that fateful Sunday, 3rd September, when war was declared. Reports included the progress on constructing the Corporation Electricity Department's new offices and showrooms in Wellesley Road, the digging of foundations for the Croydon Gas Company's new offices and showrooms on the corner of Katharine Street and Park Lane, and controversy over council plans to sell the Public Halls before new halls had been provided at Fairfield.

Residents of the Rosedene Estate and of Mitcham Road held a public meeting at Lanfranc School to protest at the corporation's proposals for a new power station at Purley Way and Croydon General Hospital was appealing for funds. Members of the Spa Hill Allotment Society were promised some reasonable security of tenure and court cases included that of six young men found guilty of insulting behaviour in the High Street. The eldest was fined 10 shillings

(50p) and the others five shillings each (25p).

Messrs Gowers advertised houses on the Spring Park Farm Estate, Shirley. These were being sold for between £845 (deposit £50 — weekly repayment 21s 9d (£1.08)) and £975 (deposit £65 — weekly repayment 24s 11d (£1.24)). A deposit of £5 secured any of these properties. Curry's in Church Street advertised Television — the miracle of the modern age; and the Southern Railway advertised an excursion to Folkestone Races by the 10.55am train from East Croydon for 12s 3d (61p) first class and 8s 2d (41p) third class.

But apart from these everyday matters it was apparent that tension was mounting. At the Southern Railway's Flower, Fruit and Vegetable Show at Waddon the General Manager told those present to "smile through the crisis". The paper also reported that everything was ready for full mobilisation of the ARP services in the town; that there had been a remarkable rush for dark material for black-out purposes; and that the scenes outside Mitcham Road Barracks were strongly reminiscent of those in August 1914.

On Sunday 3rd September 1939 war was declared. The massive evacuation, mostly of children, mothers-to-be and the blind was followed by a period of relative quiet at home which became known as the 'phoney war'. A strict black-out was imposed immediately; steps, kerbs, trees and other obstacles were white-washed or had white stripes painted on them. Vehicle lights were masked and only hand-torches covered with tissue paper to dim them could be used outdoors at night. There were numerous accidents. Sign-posts and local nameplates were removed or painted out later in 1940.

Cinemas and theatres closed but most soon re-opened with earlier times for their last performances. Many local organisations suffered as leading members were called up or found their spare time taken up with more urgent wartime activities. A great loss to the town was the closure of the well-known Croydon Repertory Theatre in Wellesley Road.

National Registration Day was 29th September. Identity cards were issued to all and were supposed thereafter to be carried at all times. The fall in local population as a result of evacuation was to some extent made up later in 1940 by a large influx of military personnel. Several temporary camps were established and some houses were requisitioned to provide accommodation for troops, European refugees and, later on for people made homeless by bombing.

Food rationing was introduced on 8th January 1940. The initial weekly allowance per person was 4oz butter, 12oz sugar and 4oz bacon or ham. From March meat was rationed, but by price — 1s 10d (9p) weekly and half that for children; from

July tea was added — 2oz weekly. Later serious shipping losses between July 1940 and June 1941 resulted in a further scarcity of supplies and the meat allowance was reduced, with only 1oz cheese permitted. Milk, fish, jam and onions became scarce and other changes to the rations occurred later and after the war. There were no ready-cooked/processed foods at this time and most households depended on basic commodities for home baking etc. A 'Black Market' developed and many tradespeople kept scarce items 'under the counter' for favoured and regular customers. Dried milk, dried eggs and dried bananas became common but were never very popular. Beer was in short supply, pubs closed early, and sometimes even had to display a notice — 'no beer'.

Construction of shelters continued and miniature forts of concrete and iron with massive walls and slit openings for firing were built at strategic points, mainly to the south of the town. Concrete blocks and barbed wire defences were sited at places where it was thought the enemy might pass or attempt to land aircraft.

Gradually many of the evacuees drifted back to the town and most of those schools which had closed were reopened. But the Battle of Britain was imminent and orders were issued for all householders to clear their lofts for safety reasons and house-to-house checks ensured this was done. On the night of 17th/18th June 1940 the first bombs to fall on Croydon, and indeed in the London area, exploded fairly harmlessly on farmland at Addington. On 3rd July a bomb fell at Riddlesdown and in August the onslaught began.

It was inevitable that Croydon would be in the thick of the battle, with its own famous aerodrome, by then in RAF service, and key RAF fighter stations at Kenley and just over the Kentish border at Biggin Hill. The battle raged overhead for several weeks, with the clear blue skies filled with vapour trails and the sound of planes in combat. On 15th August Croydon Airport was attacked before the air-raid warning had sounded. Between that day and the end of the year Croydon experienced 399 alerts — nearly three daily! Some of the raids were short but some lasted between eight and twelve hours and many bombs fell on the town. However there was little locally to compare with the devastation wrought upon the City of London and the London docks, and on town centres such as those of Coventry, Southampton and Plymouth. Air raids continued at intervals through to May 1941 by which time in Croydon 362 people had been killed and 672 sent to hospital; 1,099 houses had been destroyed, 2,655 had been sufficiently badly damaged to be unusable without major repairs and 23,000 had received some damage. These figures exclude the Urban District of Coulsdon and Purley.

Once the Battle of Britain and the Blitz were over there were only comparatively minor raids and it was not until the Flying Bomb attacks in 1944 that another concentrated bombardment occurred (see pages 25–29).

Many economies had to be made during the war and fuel such as petrol was in particularly short supply. A few motor cars could be seen on the streets with large gas bags on the roof thus avoiding the severe petrol restrictions. However these were not very successful partly due to problems with vehicle stability. Some buses were converted to gas operation using a trailer which burnt coke. The local route 197 from Norwood Junction to Caterham Valley used this method in early 1944 but acceleration was impaired and the irregular service caused complaints. They were nicknamed locally 'Baked Potato Cans'. An important local initiative was the conversion of many corporation vehicles to run on methane gas processed from the Sewage Works at Beddington.

The presence of large numbers of service personnel in and around the town, especially Canadian soldiers and local men and women of all services on leave or off-duty, meant that cinemas, theatres, dance halls and public houses were very well patronised. Not surprisingly there were occasional incidents of rowdyism, fights and drunkeness. Military parades and inspections took place frequently and there were big parades in support of the various savings and other campaigns. As an example, in Salute the Soldier Week in 1944, the *Croydon Times* reported that an estimated half a million people had watched the two-mile procession through the town on Saturday 13th May. The streets were bedecked with the flags of the Allied Nations and there were many Canadian and American troops in the crowd. Fighter planes returning from a patrol over the Channel circled the town and the seven bands in the procession included those of the Welsh Guards, the Royal Air Force, the East Yorkshire Regiment and the Metropolitan Police, while the band of the Royal Marines, Chatham, entertained the crowds in Katharine Street. The aim of the Week was to raise sufficient National Savings in the town to equip a tank regiment.

A strong sense of purpose united most of the nation, but human nature always demonstrates some less desirable attributes. Early in the war the local papers included reports of vandalism to, and theft of equipment from, air raid shelters, and later of looting from bomb-damaged property, of deserters and of people evading war work. The war, inevitably, caused great social stress — families and marriages broke up, there was widespread absenteeism amongst mothers forced into war work and torn by family duty, and some people suffered long-term psychological effects, apart from the physical disabilities caused by the bombing.

By 1945, Croydon and its people had undergone a great deal and it was to be some years before any semblance of normality returned to everyday life; in several ways, indeed, pre-war habits, customs and attitudes never returned. In particular the part played by women in the war effort ensured their position in society would be very different in future. This book illustrates the story of Croydon in the traumatic days of the Second World War and in the uncertain times that followed immediately afterwards and to the end of the 1950s.

---

4   Lorne Avenue, Shirley — 1939 *(right)*
The early weeks of the war saw intensive training on the part of the ARP services. Here an exercise in dealing with incendiary bombs is watched by volunteers and local residents.

3   Anderson Shelters *(below)*
These were named after Sir John Anderson, who as Lord Privy Seal dealt with Air Raid Precautions. They were sectioned, corrugated steel structures, about six feet six inches (two metres) long, with semi-circular roof and vertical ends. They were usually sunk about three feet (one metre) into the ground and extended about four feet six inches (one and a half metres) above it. The entrance was at one end, just about big enough for a portly person to get through if doubled up, and protected by an earth bank or perhaps a nearby wall. The tops were covered with earth for protection and to give insulation. Attractive flower beds or vegetable patches were quite often laid out on top.

This photograph shows the erection of one of some 7,500 such shelters that were put up in Croydon gardens.

5 Local Defence Volunteers – Summer 1940 (centre)

A parade of Local Defence Volunteers passes Thornton Heath Clock Tower. Soon and much more commonly known as the Home Guard (and in recent years nicknamed Dad's Army), the force was formed on 14th May 1940. This was four days after the invasion by the Germans of France, Holland and Belgium. It was open only to men between the ages of 17 and 65.

The purpose was defence of the locality against attack by German invaders, including parachutists. The volunteers made up in enthusiasm what they lacked in equipment – especially at first when there were three men to each rifle.

Z Metropolitan Zone (coincident with Z Division of the Metropolitan Police) extended from Warlingham to Streatham and from Wallington to Shirley. It was commanded by a retired Tank Corps Major, Norman Gillett, under the supervision of a retired Brigadier-General, Nelson G. Anderson who was succeeded by Colonel Ambrose Keevil. Some 30,000 men served in the Zone at one time or another.

From 25th May 1940 observation posts were manned each night and, the following day, arms, ammunition and uniforms were issued, priority being given to the southern and eastern approaches to the town.

In due course, the training and the weaponry made the force one that could, if called upon, have given a good account of itself. In the absence of any invasion, however, the Volunteers became much involved in assistance during air raids (including the manning of anti-aircraft guns). The force was 'stood down' in November 1944 (see illustration number 66, page 30).

6 ARP Recruiting Campaign – about 1939

ARP wardens were recruited from 1935 onwards and various recruiting drives such as this one took place. The photograph was taken at the west end of Woodside Green, the incomplete uniforms and number of schoolchildren watching indicating that the war had not yet started.

In 1939 the Warden service was organised under a Chief Warden, Group Head Wardens, (later known as District Wardens), Report or Post Wardens and, beneath them, the large body of wardens, whole time and part time, most of whom were volunteers and unpaid. When an 'Alert' was sounded two wardens remained at each post, the remainder going out on patrol. Gas warnings would have been given by means of rattles. Wardens checked the wind direction at sunset, advised and if necessary reported black-out infringements, and advised on the care of gas masks and measures for protecting people and property. They also manned and supervised public shelters and when the bombing started were in the forefront of the Civil Defence services, notifying the Report Centres of bomb incidents, reporting on progress made in rescue work, the state of roads and public services, and tackling incendiary bombs. They were often first into the debris of dangerous buildings to bring out casualties and to render first aid. Their contribution was tremendous.

5

War 1939 – 1945

7 Setting up a Wardens Post
This illustrates work in progress at Whitworth Road, South Norwood. Family and neighbours all seem to be involved and are just about to have the inevitable tea break.

Note the sandbags around the bay windows and the brown paper strips on the large windows, intended to reduce damage and injury from flying glass. Scenes such as this were commonplace in the early days of war. The railings had as yet not been removed but would soon disappear to be melted down, ostensibly to make munitions. Much of the metal collected for scrap to help the war effort was, in fact, unsuitable and was never used for its intended purpose.

8 Mobile First Aid Unit
A team of nurses pictured here with their Mobile First Aid Unit, part of the local ARP Auxiliary Ambulance Service. Note the windows of the building in the background (probably one of the local hospitals) protected by sandbags.

9 Merchant Navy Comforts – 1942
Many parades and special 'weeks' were arranged in the war to raise funds for a variety of purposes. The Merchant Navy Comforts Fund was organised by the Mayor, Alderman Harding, in 1942. Here he poses with the crew (part of the Heavy Rescue Service) of the *S.S. Liberty*, apparently a corporation lorry disguised as a merchant ship. It is appropriately posed alongside the lake in Wandle Park, then still reasonably full of water. The 'ship' toured the town; and with other activities the Week raised 3,000 guineas (£3,150).

MORALE

HOW TO PLAY YOUR PART

Forget yourself in helping your neighbours

In days of tension this casts out your own fears and worries. Help them to carry out all instructions about air-raids, evacuation, rationing and waste.

Keep the moral standards of the nation high

Don't weaken the home front by trying to wangle something for yourself on the quiet. Make a break with all the personal indulgence, selfishness and private wars which undermine national morale and unity. Everybody has his part to play in the moral re-armament of the nation.

Be a rumour-stopper

Those who love their country sacrifice the luxury of being the ones to pass on the "news." Any patriot shoots a rumour dead on sight. Face the facts, but don't exaggerate them. Prepare to meet them instead. Faith, confidence and cheerfulness are as contagious as fear, depression and grumbling.

The secret of steadiness and inner strength

is to listen to God and do what He says. God speaks directly to the heart of every man and woman who is prepared to listen and obey. Write down the thoughts He gives you. His voice can be heard wherever you are—in the home, in the factory, in the air-raid shelter, in the first-aid post.

Forearm yourself by listening to God first thing every morning

This provides a clear plan for each day and the power to work with other people in complete unity. In a time of listening God takes away fear and fortifies against uncertainty, hardship or bereavement; He gives foresight and cool judgment; He offers limitless reserves of energy and initiative.

A British General who has fought through two wars said this : ''Telephone wires may be cut, wireless stations be destroyed, but no bombardment can stop messages from God coming through if we are willing to receive them. To listen to God and obey Him is the highest form of national service for everybody everywhere.''

Mayor of Croydon

This message was inserted as a full page in the Croydon Times on Saturday, 20th July, 1940, by a number of Croydon business firms, as their contribution to the Nation in an hour of crisis. Further copies may be obtained from the office of the Croydon Times.
PLEASE PUT THIS UP IN YOUR HOME, OFFICE OR FACTORY

10 Propaganda

The Ministry of Information published much propaganda material on a variety of subjects. Posters bore slogans such as 'Careless talk costs lives', 'Is your journey really necessary?', 'Go by shanks's pony' (i.e. walk), 'Grow more vegetables' and 'Lend to defend the right to be free'.

Radio broadcasts similarly gave general encouragement, but the enemy used the same medium, as well as dropping leaflets from planes. The hated Nazi propagandist, William Joyce, commonly known as 'Lord Haw Haw' was regularly heard on Hamburg Radio. On 26th October 1939 he offered the grim warning: ''Croydon must beware. She is the second line of defence. We know the aerodrome is camouflaged but we know just what kind of camouflage it is. We shall bomb it and bomb it to a finish and would advise people there to evacuate the area this weekend, as we shall do the job thoroughly. But we shall be merciful and only use incendiary bombs.'' No such raid took place at that time.

There were also local initiatives. This message was first published as a full page advertisement in the *Croydon Times* on 20th July 1940, sponsored by some local businesses. It was reprinted as a poster for display in homes, offices and factories, and the newspaper reported on 27th July that its office had been besieged for copies. Some 50 years later the message highlights the changes in social attitudes which have occurred in the intervening period. It is interesting to speculate on the effect such words might have in the 1990s.

A Schoolboy in the War

I have only hazy impressions of events leading up to September 1939, except that the family were on holiday with Aunty Lil and Uncle Will at Roundhay, near Leeds. Suddenly we had to return home to South Norwood after only a few days as my mother was to help with the expected evacuation of schoolchildren from Cypress Road School which I attended.

We lived in Whitehorse Lane on the Elm Park Estate, near the corner of Nugent Road. My parents had moved there when the houses had been built in 1927. We knew many of the neighbours in Nugent and nearby Dixon and Elm Park Roads. Most of them had arrived when the estate was built and were of similar age to my parents and likewise had children. People seemed not to move house nearly so frequently in those days.

Sunday 3rd September was bright and sunny. In very sombre mood we listened to the wireless and to those fateful words of Neville Chamberlain — ''. . . and consequently we are at war with Germany''. Within a few minutes the air raid sirens sounded and we sat nervously awaiting events. Soon the 'all clear' sounded — it was a false alarm.

The following day Mother took me, a seven year old, suitably labelled and complete with small suitcase and gas mask, to the school for evacuation. As we got ready my mother came to tell me she would not after all be going with us, as intended, as a helper. At this I rebelled, threw a tantrum, burst into tears and refused to go which must have been rather unsettling for the rest of my class!

As Cypress Road School then closed, my parents sent me to a private school at 205 Selhurst Road on the corner of Upper Grove, and run by Miss Peggy Norton Collins. School here was only in the mornings and I was the sole boy. I had a somewhat miserable existence as the girls tormented and sometimes even bullied me. After some months Cypress reopened on a half-time basis and for a while I went there in the afternoons but, much to my disgust, had to continue attending at Miss Norton Collins' in the morning.

Gas masks had to be carried at all times and parents were encouraged to include emergency rations in the case. Usually these consisted of packets of nuts and raisins, and barley sugar. I managed to create imaginary emergencies nearly every day; these invariably necessitated the consumption of the raisins, which I preferred to nuts. Meanwhile at home I was very proud of the coated board on a post which had been put up in our front garden and would change colour as a warning to the locality if there were a gas attack. Later we had a stirrup pump and buckets of sand and water in the front porch for use against incendiary bombs. It was my task to keep the water replenished. Wooden shutters were put up every night in our living room partly as black-out, and partly as protection and strips of brown paper were stuck over all the windows in the house to prevent injury from flying glass.

Barrage balloons had been sited in many parks and open spaces. The nearest one to us was on the disused golf course by Norwood Lake. Our next-door neighbours, the Gaydons, who used to have regular musical evenings with songs around the piano, told me that the balloon was called 'Oscar'. One afternoon Oscar was struck by lightning and I watched him fall out of the sky in flames and land somewhere near Norwood Junction station. This called for some exploration and I found the cable was draped across much of South Norwood including the top of the spire of the Methodist Church. Presumably it had to be cut up in small sections for removal. Anyhow Oscar 2 soon arrived on the scene. Barrage balloons provided a lot of interest for children − I even possessed a model which was rigged up complete with winch and fine string attached to the pelmet in the living room.

The early days of the war seemed something of an anti-climax. Everyone was tense but little seemed to happen until the summer of 1940. My father had joined the newly-formed Home Guard and occasional exercises enlivened the district. It was fun to watch members hiding in front gardens and lurking behind walls. Public air raid shelters were appearing all over the place and many homes had their own; we had the area beneath our living room strengthened with wooden beams and supports. The house was built on a slope and there was about five feet (1.5 metres) clearance. Access was by means of a trap door and ladder in the corner of the room. Old curtains were put up around the walls with an old carpet on the floor, a bunk for me, and several camp beds for family and friends. An escape hatch led to a passage under the back garden terraces of the line of houses and until our shelter was complete we used this route into the Foskett's shelter, two doors along. Occasionally during the Blitz we paid friendly visits to each other by this means.

On 15th August 1940 my friend Tony had come to tea. The noise of aircraft was heard. My father identified them as German and we rushed to the Foskett's shelter as bombs exploded on Croydon Aerodrome. Afterwards, we went up to the top of Spa Hill and joined groups of people watching the columns of smoke rising from the area around the stricken airfield − it was our first experience of an air raid. Throughout the rest of August and September the bright blue sky was streaked with vapour trails, the silvery specks of aircraft glistening in the sun, and we saw puffs of smoke from gunfire as the Battle of Britain raged overhead. In between the aerial 'dog-fights' and air raids we schoolboys eagerly hunted for souvenirs such as shrapnel and cartridge cases. One day as I was sitting in between my mother and father in the shelter, a bomb fell about 100 yards away in Dixon Road. It was the first to land nearby and the ground and house shook as in an earthquake. So did Father. ''Why is Daddy shivering?'' I asked. ''Because he's cold,'' replied Mother.

The next six months or so were most unpleasant. The Blitz followed the Battle of Britain and night after night we stayed in the shelter. My grandparents lived at Peckham where they were much worse off for they had to sleep in a very damp Anderson shelter. They came to stay with us for a few days and the night after they arrived their home was rendered uninhabitable by a landmine. Their few days' visit lasted until Grandma died in 1946 and Grandpa in 1957, and it was not until then that I again had a room to call my own! We found plenty to do in helping the war effort during those days and nights in the shelter. The main occupation was knitting squares using odd remnants of wool. These were sewn together to make quilts for the troops and Merchant Navy and later in the war I spent some months knitting a

scarf for use by my father when on Home Guard duty on the 64 rocket-gun site at Anerley. On one occasion I decided to hold an unofficial flag day in aid of the Red Cross. Having made about 100 paper Union Jacks, stuck pins in them and placed them carefully on a cardboard tray, I set off on a house to house collection around the Elm Park Estate. The reception I received was not surprisingly somewhat mixed, especially from people who did not know me!

One day at Cypress School we heard that a bomb had destroyed the Falkland Park Avenue home of a classmate, Derek Barnes. His mother, father and baby sister had been killed. We clubbed together to buy him a Meccano set − to this day I can see him standing forlornly in front of the class as he said goodbye to us and went off to a new life.

While playing with a friend in my garden one evening, we remarked on the splendidly brilliant sunset − only to realise that the red glow was in the east and was changing in colour by the second. The London Docks were on fire and we joined a small but awestruck crowd at the top of Cypress Road to watch perhaps the greatest fire seen in England this century. That night was one of the worst of the Blitz.

Children tend to adapt their play patterns to reflect contemporary events. My friends and I were no exception. Toys were difficult to obtain but those we did get were models of such things as army lorries and tanks. My friend Tony and I enjoyed making buildings out of playing cards and bombing them with a well-aimed nutmeg. Even better, his father allowed us to use a patch of ground at the bottom of their garden in Wharncliffe Gardens to build villages. These consisted mainly of bricks, broken tiles and small pieces of wood with matchstick fences. We enjoyed bombarding these with large clods of earth taken illicitly from the better tended parts of the garden, and we had one or two lovely fires.

In 1942 I went on to Selhurst Grammar School, and found myself in form 1K with the kindly K. M. King as Form Master. His diaries provide the vivid descriptions to be found on pages 17 and 25 to 28 of this book.

Shelters were being built as the school had only just returned to Croydon after evacuation to Bideford, but raids were few and far between by that time. However lessons were occasionally disrupted and had to continue by candlelight in the air raid shelters. I was made Form Salvage Steward and enthusiastically helped the war effort by collecting books and papers. On Saturday mornings several of us would collect a barrow from the Salvage Shop in Whitehorse Road and scour the neighbourhood for metal, tin cans and anything suitable that we could scrounge from local houses or tradespeople. In 1943 the lawns in front of the school were dug up for use as allotments but my fingers were not very green. A few carrots and radishes seemed to be the only result of a lot of hard work.

After school on Friday afternoons I would usually walk through The Crescent and catch a 654 trolleybus to South Norwood Clock Tower and meet my mother. She brought sandwiches for tea which we consumed whilst watching the latest films at the *Odeon* in Station Road. On winter evenings when we came out of the cinema it was extemely difficult to see which bus to board in the black-out. The 68A and 75 buses both waited outside the station but, if no conductor was there to ask, we had to get on board and shine our dim torches at the faretable to see whether we were on

the right bus.

At school on 6th June 1944 we gathered excitedly around the radiogram (a combined wireless set and gramophone) in the hall to hear the news of D-Day; and a few days later the first flying bombs arrived. We spent most of the first night sitting in the shelter and waiting for an all-clear that did not come. It was somehow different and rumours were going around about a secret weapon. Soon we knew the worst and the next few weeks were grim indeed. On most days the nasty stuttering sound of approaching doodlebugs was heard every few minutes. Would its engine cut out or not? A sense of foreboding which only left us as the awful machine passed overhead, or increased during the silence between the time the engine cut out and the deafening, shaking explosion which followed if it landed nearby. Gradually most of the windows in the front of our house were blown out, several ceilings were partly down, and many tiles were off the roof. One day I had to make at least three visits to the nearest incident post to obtain laths and tarred material to cover up broken windows.

The neighbourhood echoed daily to explosions near and far, and the constant noise of hammering, sweeping, shovelling and the crashing of broken glass as people cleared their homes of debris. Corporation lorries maintained frequent and regular trips to clear the heaps of rubble which daily appeared outside our houses. School was disrupted and we were instructed not to leave home until at least an hour after the all-clear had sounded. When we did get to school the journey home was always beset with the thought 'will house and family still be there?'

In mid-July my parents sent me away to Paignton to stay with friends. It was the worst journey of my life. My Aunty Doris and I went by bus to Camberwell Green and there caught another bus for Paddington. On the way we passed many scenes of devastation and heard approaching and exploding doodlebugs. Paddington station was crowded beyond belief. We queued and fought our way on to the train, eventually managing to squeeze into the corridor connection between two carriages where we sat on our cases. An injured man, his head swathed in bloodstained bandages pleaded to be allowed in and so we all crowded together a little more. The journey seemed endless − nearly four hours to Exeter.

Eventually we arrived at Paignton but were not allowed off the station until our identity cards had been checked and we had provided proof that we had an address to go to. Torbay was a 'Restricted' area. The next few weeks were idyllic and peaceful, the only worry being that no news came from home for several weeks and we were not on the telephone. However all was well and early in September I returned home. The bombardment had all but ceased although the V2 rockets caused concern for a while, and occasional distant explosions were a reminder that we were still at war.

Then came VE Day and within three months, VJ Day, and a great sense of relief and rejoicing. The news was greeted by loud and continuous hooting and whistling of steam engines and electric trains at Norwood Junction and Selhurst. Next day I happily joined the crowds outside the Town Hall and also enjoyed dancing with the happy throng in Thornton Heath High Street.

The war was over. For a young person it was the experience of a lifetime, a period of excitement and danger. It was a time none of us can forget. It was also a time of fear and of sadness. I was fortunate. An uncle lost his life in the RAF but otherwise I knew only a few people who were badly affected. Many people lost everything, but anyone who lived through it was profoundly influenced by the experience and hoped it would never be repeated.

J. B. Gent

11 ARP Wardens

Some of the wardens of E 36 Post which had its headquarters in a brick-built structure behind James's tobacconists and newsagents shop on the corner of Wright's Road and Whitehorse Lane, South Norwood. The shop was owned by Melbourne Davis (later to become a local councillor). The group includes in the back row, fourth from left, Melbourne Davis, extreme right, Billie Williamson (of Nugent Road); front row, third from left W. J. Minter (Chief Warden), fourth, Stanley Crosier (of Canham Road) and fifth, Horace Foskett (of Whitehorse Lane) whose dog, Prince, is in the centre. On the extreme right is Joan Godwin, later the wife of Reg Prentice MP.

12 Barrage Balloons

These were sited on open spaces and usually remained on the ground unless air raids were expected. They were 64 feet (20 metres) long and 25 feet (8 metres) in diameter. Their cables made it difficult for enemy aircraft to make low-level attacks. During the Flying Bomb attacks in 1944 they were moved to sites along the North Downs and further out, where they made a splendid sight in the summer skies and prevented a number of bombs reaching their target, but understandably were not popular with people living in the locality.

13 Crystal Palace Tower — Wednesday 16th April 1941

Some concern was expressed locally that the towers of the Crystal Palace (almost all that remained after the 1936 fire) were a useful landmark for German aircraft and also a danger to the neighbourhood if struck by bombs. The South Tower, adjacent to Anerley Hill was demolished gradually, but the North Tower was sufficiently far from houses and roads to be demolished by explosives, as shown here. It was stated that the metal from the towers would be used in the war effort but there is no record that this was so. The tower was demolished at 12.30 pm. That night Bromley and Croydon experienced their worst air raids which suggests the Luftwaffe did not need it as a landmark.

14 Allotments at Selhurst Grammar School — 1943

This photograph was published in the *Croydon Times* of 13th February 1943. The Headmaster, Mr W. F. (Bill) Turner watches as the school gardener, aided by some boys, digs up the lawns fronting the school in The Crescent. This was part of a new campaign to encourage schoolchildren and housewives to help the Dig for Victory campaign. It was intended that the vegetables produced here would supply the school dining room.

15 Anniversary Dinner – Tuesday 9th April 1940

The Coulsdon and Purley Urban District Council was formed in 1915 and held its 25th Anniversary Dinner in the panelled upper room of the *Red Lion* at Coulsdon. Local newspapers reported many events such as this arranged by local companies and organisations at this time which indicates that life had returned to a slightly more settled pattern during the so-called phoney war. Only 24 hours later any complacency was shattered with the invasion of Norway and Denmark.

16 Addington Road, Selsdon – 1941

Selsdon raised over £1,500 in National Savings during October 1941 to buy a Bren Gun Carrier. As a mark of appreciation, on Saturday 29th November a similar machine that had seen service in Norway gave rides to local children including Diane and Richard Little (front left) and Pam Ockleford (front right). Some shops windows are boarded up as a result of bomb damage.

17 Heavy Rescue Gang about 1940

A Coulsdon and Purley UDC lorry is seen in use by a Heavy Rescue Gang in a Purley car park.

18 Croydon Aerodrome – late January 1940

January 1940 saw a record-breaking spell of cold weather which was claimed to be the worst for 73 years. From 1st to 26th of the month the aerodrome was icebound. The town had an average of 10 inches (25 centimetres) of snow with some deep drifts and with local railway lines blocked. In this view snow is being cleared from the airfield and a Blenheim, probably of 92 Squadron, is warming up its engines. It is recorded that after a four inch snowfall on the night of 27th January, a party of officers set off for Box Hill to go tobogganing only to find there was no snow there!

19 Croydon Aerodrome – 1940

Airmen of 615 Squadron cooked, ate and slept near their aircraft. Here Aircraftsman Lloyd gives a haircut alongside a Gloster Gladiator. It was March 1940 before modern Hurricanes and Spitfires arrived at Croydon.

20 Messerschmitt at Fairfield – 1940

The Croydon Fighter Plane Fund was opened in mid-July 1940 to raise £5,000 for a plane which would be called 'Croydon' and bear the borough coat of arms. To help the fund the Air Ministry loaned a Messerschmitt which had been shot down that summer in a Surrey cornfield. Its badly-wounded pilot was able to land it before dying. It was displayed at Fairfield Car Park for 10 days in late August and some 26,000 people paid to see it. Admission was 6d for adults and 3d for children.

This postcard was produced by the *Croydon Times* in aid of the fund. Note that no location is given but the Fire Station in Park Lane is visible in the background.

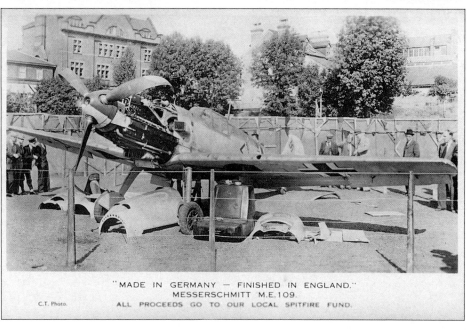

"MADE IN GERMANY – FINISHED IN ENGLAND."
MESSERSCHMITT M.E.109.
ALL PROCEEDS GO TO OUR LOCAL SPITFIRE FUND.

C.T. Photo.

21 Civil Defence Inspection — Wednesday 16th April 1941

Admiral Sir Edward (Teddy) Evans (1880–1957) photographed at Fairfield Car Park on the occasion of a spectacular ARP demonstration by over 1000 men and women representing every branch of the organisation. He was one of the most famous naval officers of his generation, a household name, known as 'Evans of the Broke' after the name of his ship which rammed a German destroyer bombarding Dover harbour in 1917. He was made an admiral in 1936 and became Regional Commissioner for London's Civil Defence in the Spring of 1939.

22 Air raid damage at Waddon — August 1940

It was a sunny evening just before 7.00 pm on Thursday 15th August 1940 when a group of German aircraft broke away from a large enemy force and attacked Croydon Aerodrome before the Alert could be given. Some bombs fell on the airfield but the main damage was to the adjacent factory area where the premises of Redwing Aircraft and British NSF were almost destroyed and others badly damaged. On the Waddon estate bombs fell in Crowley Crescent and Coldharbour Way, with fatal casualties, and in Foss Avenue and Waddon Way. In total 62 people died, and 37 were seriously, and 137 less seriously, injured. Shelter had to be found for 180 people who had been made homeless.

23 Mitcham Road Cemetery — Saturday 17th August 1940

On the day after the raid on the aerodrome, Sir John Anderson, Minister of Home Security, visited the scene and discussed the situation with the Mayor, the ARP Committee and Council officers. The Mayor opened a fund for the victims' relatives. The funeral seen here took place with burial of the unidentified victims in a mass grave. It was conducted by the Bishop, The Rt Rev Maurice Harland, as sirens were sounding and fighters were in action overhead.

24 Air raid on Kenley – Sunday 18th August 1940

Kenley Aerodrome assumed an important role early in the war with responsibility for the air defence of much of south-east England. On 18th August 1940 a serious enemy attack resulted in great damage, destruction of hangars and 10 aircraft, damage to six more aircraft and much loss of life.

This photograph was taken from Bramley Avenue, Coulsdon, with St Andrew's Church in the foreground. A heavy pall of smoke rises from Kenley. The *Red Lion* public house is the gabled, half-timbered building seen to the right of the church. Messrs Hall & Company's quarry and lime works (now an industrial estate) are by the chalk cliff.

25 Pilots at Kenley – Autumn 1940

Three of the 'Few' from 452 Squadron, Royal Australian Air Force, stand in front of a Spitfire. They are, from left to right Flight Commanders Keith ('Bluey') Truscott, DFC and Bar, Brendan ('Paddy') Finucane, DFC and Bar, and Ray Thorold Smith, DFC. Paddy Finucane is using a stick as a result of an accident in the black-out following a relaxing evening at the *Greyhound* in Croydon. Within a year or so of this photograph being taken all three had lost their lives.

26 Static Water Tank

Fire was a major worry for the Civil Defence authorities. Water mains could be broken by high explosive bombs and there was thus an urgent need for large volumes of water to be available in high risk areas. Emergency static water tanks and reservoirs were constructed in open spaces and on bomb sites. This one is in a quiet side street – Windmill Grove, at the back of houses in Forster Road. Although the main fire bomb attacks were in late 1940, the installation of tanks in Croydon did not start until late 1941.

13

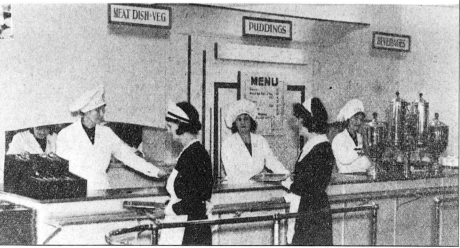

27 Public Shelter at Thornton Heath – 1940

Apart from the Anderson shelters for the garden, and the Morrison table shelters for the home, numerous public shelters were available around the town. Shops and factories also provided shelters. Here some residents of Thornton Heath enjoy a Christmas party in somewhat cramped conditions in a public shelter at Woodville Road.

28 Civic Restaurants – 1941

The idea of Civic, or British, Restaurants was launched in 1941 by Lord Woolton, the ebullient Minister of Food. The aims were to save food and fuel in the home, to free over-pressed workers from the need to prepare meals individually, to provide hot, nourishing meals at low prices and – in the event of concentrated air raids – to feed large numbers of homeless people. The restaurants were invaluable for men whose families had been evacuated, for workers who could not afford the more conventional restaurants and for working mothers and their children.

This illustration shows the first in Croydon (and in the London area). It was in Whitehorse Road near the *Gloucester* and is seen on the opening day, Monday 3rd March 1941. This may explain the presence of waitresses as these restaurants were provided with counters for cafeteria-style service though this was not common at that time. Eventually 20 buildings in Croydon (excluding the Coulsdon and Purley area) were operating, each with space for between 150 and 200 customers. They provided a midday and evening meal on weekdays, and in some cases a midday meal on Sundays. Initial prices were soup 2d, meat and two vegetables 6d, sweet 2d and tea or coffee 1½d. A lower charge was made for children.

The Whitehorse Road restaurant catered mainly for industrial workers; others like that in Mason's Avenue for shoppers. Demand fell away when the war ended and the local Civic Restaurants had all closed by 1947.

One of the Civic Restaurant patrons was an eight-year-old pupil of Davidson Infant School. Four times in 1943 he was caned (a total of nine strokes) by his Headmistress, for such offences as 'bad behaviour at Civic dinner', 'throwing salt at junior girl', 'playing truant in the afternoon following attendance at the Civic Restaurant' and 'stealing two knives from the Civic Restaurant'.

29 Summer Holidays at Home – 1942
(opposite page – above left)
30 Entertainments – 1943 *(opposite page – above right)*

In 1942 the Government asked local authorities to provide events to persuade people to spend their holidays at home thus reducing demand for hard-pressed railway and other transport services. Croydon established an Entertainments Committee under the chairmanship of Alderman James Marshall. The North End Hall, by this time war-damaged, was rented and repaired and, as the Civic Hall, became the venue for various entertainments.

32 The Rendezvous – August 1943

Perhaps typical of the way in which ad hoc arrangements were made during those wartime days, this open-air stage was set up in Thornton Heath High Street for a children's concert in aid of prisoners of war. Note the Victory 'V's above the canopy.

31 Salute to Stalingrad Festival – 1943
A fund was established to provide clothing, blankets and medical supplies for the people of Stalingrad who were resisting the German army so valiantly. Alderman Sam Roden, the Mayor, gave it a good send off at the *Grand Theatre* on Wednesday 30th January. Several 'Russian Droskhkys' (adapted from corporation vehicles) toured the town as fund raisers. Then a Grand Civic Ball was held on Wednesday 17th March at Kennards. It included a stage appearance by Tommy Trinder and raised £1,400; eventually some £8,000 was sent to Russia to provide a 'Croydon' ward in a new hospital in Stalingrad.

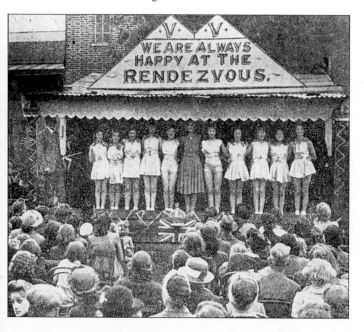

33 Gillett and Johnston's Bell Foundry
Nowadays this would be described as a 'photo opportunity'. The illustration shows Stafford (later Sir Stafford) Cripps, the austere Minister of Aircraft Production, visiting the Whitehorse Road premises of the famous bell founders. During the war the firm took on 450 extra workers and, as in the First World War, concentrated on the production of fuses, pistols and gas warning bells.

34 Selhurst Carriage Cleaning Shed – October 1940
Railways were frequent targets for enemy attack. Apart from their obvious strategic importance they were fairly easy to identify from the air by day, or on moonlit nights, or with the aid of flares. Railway installations in the Croydon area received frequent damage and disruption. The valiant efforts of the vital transport staff in keeping things going are well recorded in *War on the Line* by Bernard Darwin and *London Transport at War* by Charles Graves.

35 Croydon Bus Garage – May 1941
On the night of 10th/11th May eight high explosive bombs fell in the vicinity of the *Red Deer* at South Croydon. One landed on an Anderson shelter causing four deaths. Another hit the polishing store of the Camco Works in Sanderstead Road, and two fell on the London Transport bus garage. Many of the vehicles had their tanks full of petrol and devastation ensued. Sixty five buses were completely destroyed or damaged beyond repair. Heroic efforts were made to rescue trapped staff and Henry Lock Kendell of Blenheim Park Road, the Commandant of Stretcher Depot 8 at nearby St Augustine's Hall later received a Royal Commendation for his bravery. He found a bus on top of an inspection pit on fire; some staff were in the pit or had been blown under other buses. He rescued three of them and returned four times while the Fire Brigade played water which scalded him when it splashed him, such was the heat. He was later Mayor (1958 to 1960) and died in 1987.

The picture shows the garage on the morning after the incident.

A night in the Blitz

37   North End − 1941

North End on a rather dismal December day. Wilson's Café on the left was a popular meeting place for Croydonians for over 70 years. The aroma of freshly-roasting coffee usually wafted across North End and must have been a comforting reminder of better times. Crown House and Barclays Bank now occupy the site while Kennards famous store has been replaced by the Drumond Centre. Note the small 'starlight' fittings under the globes of the street lights. These gave a tiny glimmer of light to relieve the density of the black-out.

36   K. M. King and the night of 16th/17th April 1941

The Blitz on London and the South East lasted from August 1940 to May 1941. In Croydon, following a month of comparative quiet the air raid siren sounded at 9.03 pm on Wednesday 16th April 1941.

An incendiary bomb attack on the region started shortly afterwards, and the sound of attacking enemy dive bombers, exploding bombs, and gunfire continued until 4.00 am. The local Fire Brigade was called to 230 fires and was also summoned to assist at fires in Beckenham and Clapham. Three parachute mines caused severe damage. One wrecked much of the Queen's Road Homes. Another fell in Limes Avenue, Waddon, and wrecked or damaged every house in that road and in Lodge Avenue, Wandle Side, Waddon Court Road, Mill Lane, and in Purley Way from Alton Road to Jennett Road. A third caused great damage in and around Court Drive, Waddon. Sixty other serious incidents occurred in the town and there were 12 delayed action bombs. On this one night 76 people were killed, 91 seriously and 65 slightly injured.

Kenneth Malcolm King (1898−1976), a history teacher at Selhurst Grammar School for 37 years and affectionately nicknamed 'Smiler' by his pupils, was also a local historian, author, book collector, pillar of the scout movement and something of a pioneer of trips abroad. A bachelor, he lived in The Crescent, opposite the school, with his sister, Ruby.

He kept a diary for more than 50 years, vividly recording national and local events, as well as the ups and downs of his personal life. He was also a scourge of what he saw as local injustices and gives a fascinating insight into Croydon life.

The accompanying extract from his diary describes the night of 16th/17th April 1941. Further diary extracts appear on page 25−28. They are reproduced by kind permission of Peter Byde.

Wednesday 16th April 1941

It had been a lovely day and a clear night followed, so we were not surprised when the sirens sounded soon after nightfall. Very soon it became evident that this was no minor air-raid. The barrage guns were thundering on all sides, and searchlights turned the dark into a bright, white twilight. Still, we thought it was hardly necessary to go across into one of the School shelters so we stayed in the dining-room at home, listening − Ruby rather scared − to the inferno of noise outside. Then, soon after ten o'clock, we heard a clatter which we thought was that of slates falling from the roof. I hurried to the street door and saw an astonishing sight. The noise had been that of the falling of incendiary bombs, a dozen of them, by this time blazing furiously. The first had fallen in the road, just outside the house and within 15 yards of it; the rest were at intervals of about 25 yards towards the girls' school, straddling it − three in the roadway, one in front of the school, one in the playground behind and the rest in the playing field. By this time fire parties and wardens of The Crescent and the immediate district were all rallying and in the midst of the awful spectacle their appearance was really comic: mostly women, they came running along, blowing whistles to give the alarm, and most of them carrying dust-bin lids for protection. As they ran from each direction, some of them were shouting, ''The girls' school's on fire!'' Naturally I joined in the run lest it were true and it were necessary to give access to the building: and indeed it looked as though the school were ablaze − the glow of the bombs in the field behind shone redly through the windows back and front of the building. It was astonishing that in all this shower of incendiaries (probably a 'Molotov bread-basket') not one bomb had landed on any part of the buildings. There were at least two people available to deal with each bomb, so I returned to Ruby who was watching the exciting scene from the safe cover of the front porch, and there we stayed for nearly an hour watching a display of the fireworks of war that would be described as gorgeous if it were not so sinister. Searchlights still probed the pale night sky, and against their light shells burst like rockets; in three different directions the sky was reddened with the glare of fires, smudged with columns of smoke; red tracer bullets described graceful arcs; and two groups of pale yellow flares drifted slowly down, shedding a brilliant light. It was a beautiful rather than a terrifying spectacle. There was, of course, a continuous accompaniment of sound, mainly the bursting of shells and the ringing of ambulance and fire-engine bells. Then, as we stood watching and listening, there was a sudden reddish glow, a loud explosion, and, while we still felt the movement of rushing air, the sudden tinkling of shattered glass. By now we thought it time to go indoors again, and, with the raid still in noisy progress, went to bed at midnight, Ruby preferring to sit up in a lighted room with a fire till the fury of the raid abated. This is the nearest we have been to falling bombs, and somehow I am not in the least frightened but simply exhilarated and excited − I should have been sorry to miss it.

Salvage and National Savings

38   Pram Shortage – 1942
This advertisement from the *Croydon Times* demonstrates one of the many shortages common during the war. Virtually everything was in short supply and the slogan 'Make do and Mend' applied widely.

39   Savings Shop – 15th June 1940 (above)
Croydon was a leading town in the wartime National Savings movement. Campaigns were promoted throughout the war and on 4th March 1940 the first National Savings shop in the country was opened at 72 George Street. It was provided by the Corporation free of rent and rates.

Here, during National Savings Week in June 1940 the Mayor, Alderman Harding (seated right) and the Town Clerk, Ernest Taberner (seated left) make personal purchases of savings certificates. Standing are Rear Admiral J. H. Harrison (left) and Frank Roberts, the Joint Honorary Secretaries of the local movement. Miss G. E. Morgan, Chief Voluntary Worker is seated.

The first Street Savings Group in the country was initiated in East Ward in 1940 and by the end of 1941 the town had some 1,300 groups. Croydon raised a total of £20,000,000 in National Savings between 1940 and 1945.

40   Wings for Victory Week – 1943 (below)
During Wings for Victory Week (1st to 8th May) Croydon raised £1,200,755, the cost of 240 fighter planes. The success of the Week was largely due to the efforts of members of savings groups and ordinary Croydonians such as these savings team leaders at Whitehorse Manor School. They are proudly displaying a model of a Gloster Gladiator made by 13 year old Roy Simpson (back row, centre). The model was covered with 6d savings stamps by the pupils of the school and was later on show in the shop of Harford & Sons, tailors, in Thornton Heath High Street. Included in the photograph are Colin Richardson (centre row, right of table), Brian Meech (centre row, extreme right) and John Williams (front row, left of notice board).

41   Dustmen and Volunteer Helpers
42   The Mayor's Paper Chase – 1941
43   Residents at Scrap Depot in Boston Road, Thornton Heath – August 1940
44   Kennards' Advertisement from *Croydon Times* – 1942
45   Advertisement for Salvage Book Drive – 1943 (opposite)

In November 1939 the Corporation set up a sub-committee of the Highways Committee,

which later became an independent Salvage Committee. In February/March 1940 a house-to-house canvass for waste paper, rags, bottles and bones was made. A Salvage Shop opened in George Street in May 1940 and this was soon followed by a further seven around the districts. These acted as receiving depots for scrap materials. Corporation dustmen and drivers volunteered their evenings and Saturday afternoons to collect in bulk from the depots material gathered by scouts, guides and other voluntary workers. From 1941 waste food was collected for feeding pigs and poultry (see page 22).

Various salvage campaigns were mounted, and following a national appeal by Lord Beaverbrook for waste paper, a special local effort took place in 'The Mayor's Paper Chase', the first event of its kind in the country. A street procession nearly half a mile in length led by the Mayor and including mobile tableaux, made its way from Fairfield Car Park. Schoolchildren lined the route and, as the procession passed, quantities of waste paper, old ledgers, files and documents were thrown into dustcarts. Despite precautions no doubt some documents and books of considerable interest were lost in this and similar events.

By late 1945 the local wartime campaign had produced 37,885 tons of material for recycling and this had produced revenue of £131,950.

46 Norwood Grove – 1943
Hoeing onions on parkland which had been turned over to agriculture.

47 Coombe Lodge – 1943
A tractor ploughing land at Coombe Lodge. This is now the Parks Department Central Nursery.

48 Exhibition Handbill – 1943
Numerous demonstrations and exhibitions promoted the 'Dig for Victory' campaign.

49 Norbury Station – 1940
Vegetables growing on the platform at Norbury. Note that the lights have their posts painted to aid visibility in the blackout, and that the lamps have been removed from the main line platforms (left), presumably to save fuel.

Dig f

Rationing started in January 1940, and as supplies of food from the Continent were cut farmers switched from growing vegetables to corn for bread, and other crops for animal feed. The Government encouraged everyone to grow vegetables and in August 1940 they launched an award for home vegetable production. The phrase 'Dig for Victory' was coined by a London evening paper and soon lawns, flower beds and any suitable spare piece of ground were turned over to vegetable production.

In Croydon the Parks Department made their contribution. New allotments were established and those parts of Purley Way Playing Fields not needed for a gun-site and a military camp (some

ictory

70 acres) were turned over to growing wheat and potatoes. Other parks also contributed, and the produce was sold to hospitals, the civil Restaurants, and to welfare organisations.

Local groups organised Pig, Poultry and Rabbit Clubs and many individuals kept a few hens and rabbits.

The Ministry of Food under Lord Woolton was responsible for this verse:

'Those who have the will to win,
Eat potatoes in their skin
Knowing that the sight of peelings
Deeply hurts Lord Woolton's feelings.'

50 Purley Way − 1943
A green crop growing in a fire break between the wheat on Purley Way Playing Fields. Local housewives and boys from Whitgift School helped with the harvest.

51 Purley Way − 1943
Bird scaring on the wheatfields in Purley Way.

52 Women's Land Army − 1943
53 Recruiting Campaign Poster − 1946
The Women's Land Army began recruiting in May 1939. Pay was at first about £3 weekly from which lodging expenses had to be paid. It was described as 'The Army behind the Army'. This group was in the Whit Monday Horse Parade and Carnival sponsored by Croydon Salvage Committee on 14th June 1943. An estimated 40,000 people watched the event.

The poster dates from the year after the war − a reminder of the severe food shortages which continued into the 1950s.

21

Housewife plays her part
Tipping Waste Food at plant
Emptying Concentrated Food from boiler
Concentrated Food being fed to the pigs

Street Collections
Sorting Waste Food ready for cooking
Collecting Concentrated Food
Collecting Concentrated Food

COLLECTION AND CONCENTRATION OF WASTE FOOD

54   Waste Food Collection
This shows the methods of waste food
collection and processing which commenced in
the early 1940s. Waste food bins were sited at
convenient places all around the town and
housewives were encouraged to save any
scraps for the bins. The illustration was
published in a book issued by the Council in
1946 and entitled *Our Croydon*.

55 Firewatching at the Parish Church – 1944

Following the devastation of the City of London by fire bombs at the end of 1940 it was decreed that all men between 18 and 60 were liable for enlistment as Fire Guards. They were trained to deal with incendiary bombs and to use stirrup pumps. From March 1942 women between the ages of 20 and 45 were similarly liable. The maximum amount of duty required was 48 hours per month. The activity was commonly known as 'firewatching'.

The staff of the Croydon Parish Church, and doubtless the Bishop, were trained by the Chief of the Croydon Fire Brigade, for the building was potentially a severe fire hazard. Most other Fire Guards were trained more informally. In the event, the Parish Church suffered no structural or fire damage, though some windows were blown out by a flying bomb that fell in Cranmer Road on 27th July 1944.

Here the Bishop, The Rt Rev Maurice Harland, is pictured with a group on fire watching duty in the vestry of the church early in 1944, when there were few raids and most of the duties were spent waiting rather than watching.

56 Addington – Sunday 27th June 1943

This peaceful scene was at a time when relatively little enemy action was taking place over Croydon. The church of St Mary the Blessed Virgin, dating from 1080, is seen from the grounds of Addington Palace. Its rural isolation was still evident despite the just visible encroachment of the First National Housing Trust's estate on the horizon at Castle Hill.

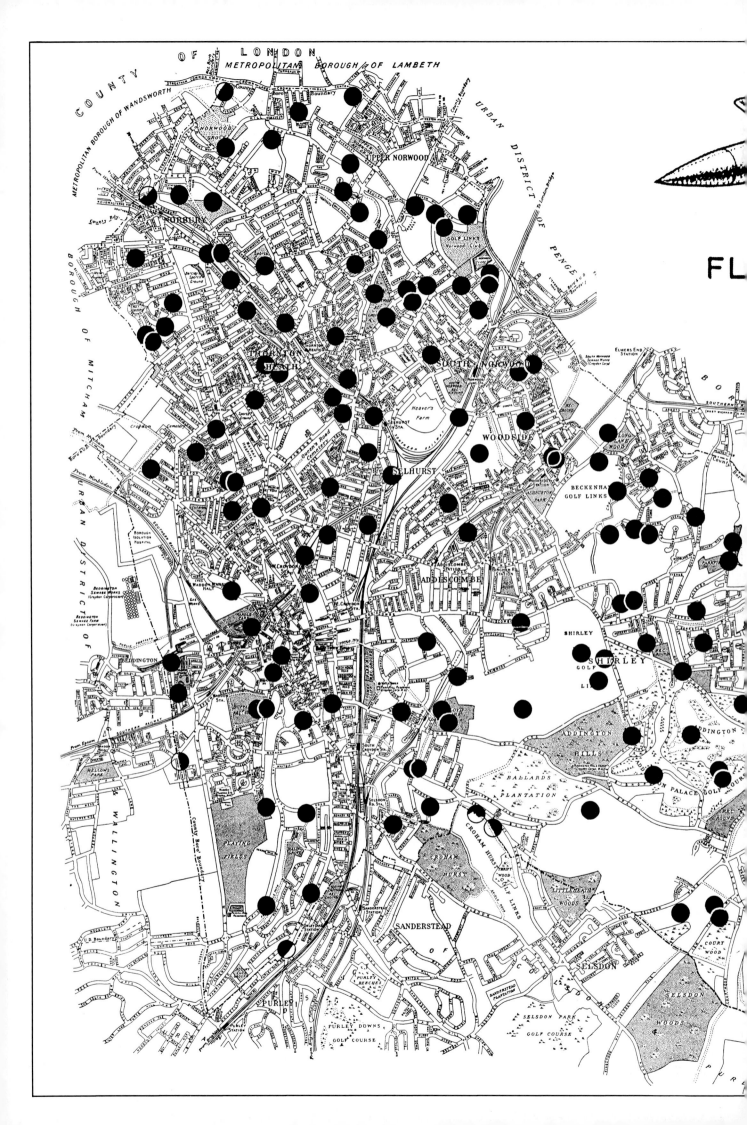

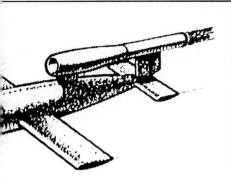

IG BOMB (V.I.)

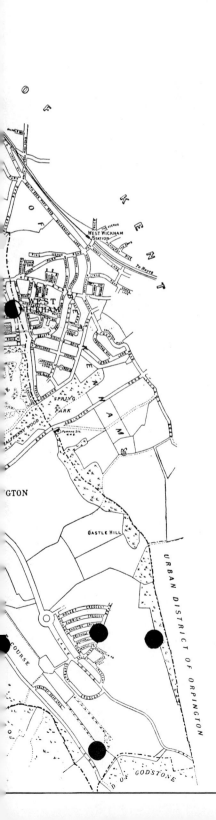

57 The Doodlebugs

For several years the Government had known that the Germans were developing a secret weapon, and air reconnaissance had revealed some launching sites. The first of the pilotless planes was launched on 13th June 1944 and for the following 80 days and nights the sinister sound of these V1s, Flying Bombs, Buzz-Bombs or Doodlebugs as they were soon nicknamed, was an all too familiar feature of life in London and south east England.

The Flying Bombs were cheap, mass-produced unpiloted bombs with rocket propulsion. They travelled between 80 and 100 miles with nearly one ton of high explosive and fell randomly when the fuel supply cut out or when brought down by fighter planes, anti-aircraft fire, or barrage balloon cables. They usually created only a small crater but did an immense amount of blast damage over a radius of about 400 yards (350 metres).

Croydon was the worst hit town, but escaped some of the most serious incidents such as those at Lewisham where one bomb killed 59 people, seriously injured 126, and slightly injured 178, or at Beckenham where 44 were killed and many more injured. Within a few weeks of the attack starting, a mass evacuation took place. Over 36,000 people left Croydon in July 1944. Long queues were a daily sight in Katharine Street as people with nowhere to go waited at the Education Office for suitable arrangements to be made for them.

To help with repairs to property, 1,500 building workers were drafted into the town from other parts of the country. They were accommodated in schools, halls and temporary huts. Eleven who came from Scotland and Ireland were killed in huts at Aurelia Road only a few hours after they arrived. One contingent from the Midlands decided the danger was too great and returned home.

The worst of the onslaught was over by mid-August 1944 but the last did not fall until the night of 14th/15th November. The map was published by the *Croydon Times* and shows where Doodlebugs fell in Croydon. Some 54 also fell in the Coulsdon and Purley area and Croydon Local Studies Library holds maps showing the location of these and of all the wartime bomb incidents in both areas.

Summer 1944
Extracts from the contemporary account in K. M. King's Diary

Saturday 17th June

We have passed through the most alarming and hectic night of the war. I went to bed at the usual time and, being very tired, slept so heavily that I was not aware of the P-plane [Pilotless-planes] raid that began just before midnight. But about 2.30 a.m. I was awakened by the collapse of part of the ceiling of my bedroom — fortunately most of the debris was clear of my bed. Ruby was already up and dressed and told me that she thought a window had been blown out. Sure enough, the two large windows in my study were gone, and as well the street-door was blown wide open. The whole atmosphere was filled with what seemed an acrid mist; it proved to be billowing clouds of dust from the wreckage made by an exploding P-plane. In the darkness it was impossible to check the extent of the damage, and, as all seemed quiet again, I went back to bed. But not for many minutes — there was another explosion, and again the noise of falling glass and rubble. This time it was a patch from the scullery ceiling and another from the lumber room and several panes of conservatory roof. It seemed useless to return to bed so I dressed and joined Ruby downstairs. When all seemed quiet and secure, I went over to the School to see how the fire-watchers were getting on, and a tragic and strange spectacle faced me. The rest room was crowded with some 40 old men, women and children, dazed and begrimed refugees from the disaster that had overwhelmed Northbrook and Pawsons Roads, streets of small working-class houses some 200 yards away, where the P-plane exploded. For want of anywhere else to go, these poor people had been sent to take refuge in the School. Nixon was busy giving first aid as necessary, and Miss Tickner and Miss Raynham [School Secretaries] were making tea for them all, but in such difficult conditions that I continued the job on the gas cooker at home.

I waited impatiently till it was light enough to start clearing up the mess of glass and ceiling rubble and take stock of the exact extent of the damage. I am thankful that we have escaped so lightly — there was the damage already enumerated, and in addition I found that the whole roof of the conservatory had been dislodged by blast to about half-an-inch of its true position. I went with Nixon to see just what has happened in the neighbourhood, and found a trail of ruin almost incredible in extent from a single explosion. Scores of panes of glass in the School windows have been broken, and a big patch of the roof stripped. In Whitehorse Road for 150 yards there is no shop-front left, most of the windows and many of the doors of the houses have been broken, and all the roofs damaged in varying degrees. But in Northbrook and Pawsons Roads the devastation was complete; though the outer walls of most of the houses were standing, doors, windows, roofs, chimneys and ceilings were all gone. I was told later that 12 people were killed — if it had been 100 I should not have been surprised. I saw George Henning who is District Warden, haggard with exhaustion and begrimed and he told me what many others said as well, that this affair was vastly worse than the last bomb disaster in Pawsons Road in 1940. The second explosion had been that of a P-plane falling in Selhurst New Road, another working-class street, and there the devastation is said to have been even worse.

Police were guarding the half-wrecked shops in Whitehorse Road till their owners could take charge, and all the householders were busy clearing the glass and rubble from their homes into piles in the streets. All the morning there was the sound of shovelling glass when lorries came to cart it away, and then men came to do 'first-aid' repairs to windows and roofs. All day long through The Crescent there was a pathetic procession of poor people with their few salvaged odds and ends piled on prams and barrows.

There were no warnings during the morning, but there were several in the afternoon, with heavy gunfire, and it is evident that people are scared by this new secret weapon to judge by the way they rushed to shelter when the sirens sounded. I am on a turn of fire-duty tonight, and all the evening there have been Alerts and gunfire, and so Ruby will spend the night in the School lest she should be scared of being alone in the house.

Sunday 18th June

We have been up most of the night. There have been eight Alerts in 14 hours, most of them lasting about half-an-hour, but the longest went on from 10 p.m. to 6 a.m. It was accompanied by such heavy gunfire for the first half of the time that in any case sleep would have been impossible. . . . We gave shelter all night to a soldier who had been given leave when he had news that his home in Northbrook Road was destroyed, but he arrived home after dark, knew nothing of the whereabouts of his family and came to us for help. We did what we could, but obviously he could do nothing in the dark, so he stayed with us until morning. . . .

Wednesday 21st June

Everything still at sixes-and-sevens with the raids of the flying bombs. . . . School attendances were very small, and most of the day had perforce to be spent in the shelters. The Coombe Road district of Croydon suffered most from the attacks during the night, and Mills is away from School with his house well-nigh destroyed. During an Alert this afternoon, rather than go into the stifling shelter, I went out into the School field, whence I could see the massed barrier of barrage balloons which is one of the expedients used to keep the things away from the London district. One of the flying bombs came in sight, streaking across the sky with an RAF plane in hot but ineffectual pursuit, and then I saw the bomb dive with a great explosion and a tall pillar of smoke and dust. It seemed to be in the direction of Grange Wood, and we heard later that it fell in Ross Road. This evening I spent some time clearing up the patch of laths where part of my bedroom ceiling fell.

Thursday 22nd June

They started early with their flying bombs this morning — between half-past six and seven o'clock when I heard five going over, but fortunately for us they came to earth too far away for us to feel the thud: and then at 8.25 a.m. another came over and landed near Norbury Station with an explosion that shook the house. The All Clear did not come till halfway through the morning, and so there were fewer boys at School than ever. In the 13 forms from the Fourth downwards, there were only four boys at School at eleven o'clock: and only 42 boys in all took dinner at School. With no classes to take, I went early into the town to bank the dinner money. The streets were strangely empty, and in the shops there were many items of food that would normally have been snapped up much earlier.

Friday 23rd June

The General Schools Examination began today. We had had the prospect of having the boys working in the corridor shelters, where they could have gone on (relatively) undisturbed by warnings: but though Turner [the Headmaster] spoke of this as probable, it would have been quite unworkable, and a plan that I suggested has been investigated and acted upon. Our examination candidates have gone to the Elmwood School to sit their exam, where they can work in two strengthened classrooms which are as safe as shelters. Four of the Staff have to be there for invigilation, and Mills and Mrs Maclean are still away on account of bomb damage to their houses — Mills's place is pretty badly wrecked. . . .

Saturday 24th June

A hot sunny day of cloudless skies, an ideal Midsummer Day, and it has had the great advantage that the clear skies make the flying bombs too good a target for our guns and planes and it is possible to detect their bases in Northern France, so all day long there has been no Alert at all. Everyone has enjoyed the respite from the strain of hearing the wretched things coming over, seeing them and wondering where they will fall. . . . I found plenty to keep me busy all day — including the best part of two hours standing in food queues. One of them was in order to get some cherries from a barrow in Surrey Street: there are no cherries in the shops, and it is said that wholesalers choose this way of selling in order to make the profit of retail prices. Also today I had a supply of gooseberries from Eva, the first I've seen this year, and I have bottled seven jars of them for the winter, and three of cherries.

Thursday 29th June

During the night there were several flying bombs that came to earth nearby and again in the early hours of this morning, one of them falling in Poplar Walk just at the time when people were on their way to work. Boys on a bus just by West Croydon Station were very near to it, but were much more excited than frightened by it. As the days pass and more districts are affected, inevitably it comes about that more of the Staff sustain damage to their houses: so far, nine of the 24 of us have suffered more or less. The two latest are Turner and Vallins, in the course of last night. A bomb fell in South Norwood Hill near Turner's house and he has lost most of his windows, ceilings and doors. Poor Vallins has suffered more heavily. Only last Thursday he moved house from Anerley to Banstead, and last night a flying bomb landed right in front of his new home. He and Mrs Vallins escaped unhurt by the fact of their being in the shelter in the garden, but the house is almost wholly wrecked: they are left with only the kitchen habitable to live in by day, with the shelter to sleep in by night — and this after only six days' occupation of their new home! We are particularly sorry for Mrs Vallins because she is such a good housewife and so house-proud and after all she can't come away from the ruin by day as Vallins can. I have been interested to hear how considerately the Croydon authorities treat people who are bombed out of their homes. Our Mrs Maclean lost all her clothing when her house was destroyed last week, and within a few days she was given 100 clothing coupons to get on with: how different from the niggardly treatment Aunt Lucy received.

By great good fortune we were able to get the dinners done with in an interval between the Alerts: and the playground shelters are more habitable now that electric light has been run out from the main building on the initiative of the 6th Form boys.

Saturday 1st July

We had a quiet night, and though the Alert was still on, we all went to bed, the ladies taking the precaution of making up their beds in the corridor shelter; but there was nothing in the locality till after daybreak this morning. And then the wretched things came over in rapid succession, favoured by low cloud. There were three big explosions round about seven o'clock, and I heard soon after that two of them were in the Ross Road area again. And this evening I found that Turner was bringing all his family to sleep in the corridor shelters at the School, because of further extensive damage to his house — the rest of the ceilings down, and all the 'first aid' repairs to his windows carried away by blast. In my opinion these makeshift window coverings are so depressing that I had my study windows reglazed yesterday; and though all my neighbours have had their fabric coverings blasted away, my panes of newly-fitted glass are still intact.

The flying bombs were still coming over with sickening monotony when I set out for my usual shopping, but it was noticeable that the streets were almost deserted, and likewise the shops. There was this compensation, however, that I was able to buy a couple of pounds of strawberries at my greengrocer's — the first we have had this year, and this was good fortune because subsequently I saw none in other shops or on the street barrows. While I was wondering whether to risk going into the town, there was the shattering of another explosion quite near. It was in another small street of working-class homes, and it presented a pitiful spectacle when I went shopping later in the morning that way. The whole road appeared to be wrecked; no windows were left in the houses nor ceilings in all the adjoining roads; and not a shop front in more than half of Thornton Heath High Street. There were no bombs while I hurried to the town and back, and only one while I was going to Thornton Heath; but they kept coming over at intervals all the afternoon, so I stayed indoors as a precaution.

Tuesday 4th July

A quiet night, but the flying bombs began coming over quite early this morning, and there has been an almost continuous Alert all day. All of School time, including the dinner-hour, was spent in the shelters, except for a scant 10 minutes in the middle of the afternoon. The All Clear was sounded, so we gave the boys the chance to stretch their legs in the playground for a 20-minute break, but the sirens sounded again halfway through. One of the bombs that fell this morning was at Norbury and Boz and Scott were summoned by telephone to go home and attend to the damage done to their houses. The enormous extent of the damage — far worse than anything we experienced in 1940−41 — was well exemplified by what I saw this morning. Last evening a bomb fell at the further end of Thornton Heath High Street, and when I had to go that way for shopping today I noticed that not a single building (house, shop, school, factory or church) is completely intact in all the way from this house to the Thornton Heath Clock, a distance the best part of a mile. This was just the visible damage; one can imagine much that can't be seen. And it was just what could be seen along the main road; in every side-street one could see fresh heaps of glass and ceiling rubble in the gutters. We seem to be getting the bombs heavily here in Croydon, but most other suburban districts of South London are as badly hit, if not more badly. . . .

Tuesday 11th July

A bright, pleasant day with no Alerts all the morning, and only one during afternoon School. But during that one, there were nine flying bombs over in less than 10 minutes. I suppose they gave our defences the slip somehow, and the number that got through in so short a time is some indication of what we might have experienced, but for the adequacy of the defences.

Then, as we were sitting at tea, another came over, flying very low, and came to earth with a tremendous crash about a quarter of a mile away. The whole house rocked with the explosion, and I had the unusual spectacle of a ripple pass over the surface of the ceiling immediately before a patch of it collapsed. Most of the room, including the tea table, was covered with rubble, but we were unhurt, though Ruby was rather shaken. At the same moment my study ceiling also crashed down, but did no damage to the bookcases; and half-a-dozen more panes of the conservatory roof fell in. We finished our tea amongst the wreckage – I did this deliberately to calm Ruby – and then I spent two busy hours making a first clearance of the debris. Just as we were more fortunate than most of our neighbours last time, so this time we have suffered more heavily. I heard that the bomb had fallen in Bensham Manor Road, near where Harding now lives, so I went (as soon as I had cleared the debris) to see if he and Mrs Harding needed somewhere to spend the night. The bomb actually fell in a small turning, Marion Road, and nine or 10 houses were completely pulverised: no semblance of a wall was standing – there was just an empty space, with a great deal of brick dust and bits of broken wood. The adjoining houses, within a radius of 100 yards, had suffered fearfully. Harding's house was standing, and that was about all. He had already gone to Anerley, for two previous bombs had made the place uninhabitable. In one partly wrecked house I saw what summed up one aspect of the whole horrid business: a tea-table had been laid for the meal, the cake, the jam, the crockery all set out, but in the midst of it a wireless set had been hurled by the blast: and there was the meal prepared but not eaten. It seemed typical of the way these senseless

58 Ross Road Incident – June 1944
A flying bomb fell in Ross Road, South Norwood, on the afternoon of Wednesday 21st June 1944, causing havoc in the area. In this photograph Mr and Mrs H. U. Willink are seen at the site, with Alan Holt, Deputy Borough Engineer in charge of the Rescue Services, on the left. Henry Willink was MP for Croydon North.

59 Damaged Shop – 1944
A queue waits patiently to be served at a bomb-damaged butcher's shop in North End. The sign 'Business as Usual' often appeared outside badly-damaged shop premises or the remains of buildings. It is many years since there was a butcher's shop in North End.

60 Emergency Street Baths
When the flying bomb attacks were at their worst, street baths such as this toured the town. The public baths had been damaged and many houses had been wrecked or severely damaged. Hundreds of people were living in shelters without washing facilities.

infernal machines cut into and across ordinary peaceful life. Whitehorse Road was like a disturbed anthill for activity − people carrying out ceiling rubble and glass, fastening up yet again the temporary coverings of their windows (which are ripped off with the blast of every new bomb) and fixing their doors afresh. The School has lost a lot more windows, including a number in the Staff Room.

Friday 14th July

Another quiet night, but just before nine o'clock this morning, there was a bomb in Saxon Road that has done tremendous damage. These flying bombs seem to vary in explosiveness, and this was one of a very heavy type: and there are other variants of type, this being a bomb of which the engine cut off long before it swooped, so that there was no warning except a slight swishing sound. I was just at the door of the School about to go home with the weekly periodicals that I had just collected from the newsagent, when there was a thud and a deafening roar that gave wings to my feet as I rushed across the road to see how Ruby was faring. I think she was very frightened, but was quickly reassured. Then I checked up on the damage − a window in the dining-room broken; two more ceilings down; and the side door burst open, with the step-ladder that usually stands against it hurled across the hall by the blast of the explosion; but I found the worst damage outside − the brick-work of the bay window of the dining-room so cracked as to be in danger of collapse if there are any more explosions so near. I had to report back to School, of course, before beginning to clear the worst of the mess, and I returned to find a shocking scene of devastation. At the back of the building, not a window is left; one main entrance door was smashed like a match box and the other was torn from its hinges. Even one of the front doors was gashed as by a hatchet; almost the whole of the back roof was a ruin of tiles and all the sky-lights gone. School was an obvious impossibility, and except for seniors who volunteered to stay and help clear up the litter of broken glass and tiles − barrowfuls of it − the boys were sent home. Greenwood and Pascoe were soon the the scene, and by mid-morning it was decided that we can't keep going and so the term will be wound up next Wednesday, instead of 28th July. In the meantime, anxiety was growing about the safety of Mrs Ashton. She was known to have come by train to Selhurst Station, and would have been due to arrive a few minutes before the bomb fell: and there was no further news of her, till at midday it was ascertained that she was seriously injured and was lying unconscious in Mayday Hospital.

I had spent most of the morning clearing up the debris at home, the house once more thick with dust everywhere. And after I had been back to School to deal with the dinner accounts for the week, I returned to carry on. I have had to go back on my determination not to have broken windows covered with black felt paper (which is issued for the purpose) and I covered the broken dining-room windows with it. I was able to tinker about with the brick-work and make it a bit more secure till the local authority can come and deal with it − Mr Whitehorn's workmen have all been commandeered for factory repairs.

This evening I had to go back to school for a turn of fire-duty, and there, from Longhurst first, confirmed in detail by Turner, I heard the shocking news of what really happened to Mrs

Ashton this morning. It was not she in the hospital at all. She was terribly injured and instantly killed in Saxon Road on her way from the station. Yet this is only on circumstantial evidence: there is an unidentified woman in the mortuary who must be Mrs Ashton. She is missing, and we know she must have been in Saxon Road just when and where the bomb fell: and a gold bangle, like the one she always wore, has been found. The police say that the body can never be identified, and it is so shockingly mutilated that they will allow no one to see it. Horrifying as this is when one thinks of Mrs Ashton's fate, the suddenness of it is some consolation as far as she is concerned, for she could have known nothing. But we are intensely sorry for poor Bill Ashton, who idealized and idolized his wife to a degree I have known in no other husband. He is likely to be broken by the tragedy.

[Mrs Marion Ashton was the wife of Selhurst teacher William Ashton, joining the school staff when he went into the Forces.]

Thursday 27th July

My salary cheque reached me by post this morning, this being the first time in 25 years that it has come to me in this way. Another departure from the normal practice is definitely unpleasing. It has always been the practice to pay us our salaries for July and August with one cheque at the end of July, and I have always planned my budget accordingly. But a circular was sent round the schools to notify the change of procedure, and the wording of it suggested that the Committee didn't want to pay the August salary in advance, lest any teachers were killed by flying bombs!

Friday 28th July

The bombs have come nearer than ever − round about midnight one landed at the other end of The Crescent. I had been asleep (in the dining-room on the floor) for some time and had been awakened by an explosion a few minutes before. As I lay in bed wondering if it was necessary to get up and investitgate, there was a sudden orange glare, a dull rumble (the bomb explosions don't seem so loud when they are comparatively close) and the following second it seemed that everything was falling. Had I judged by the moment's impression, I should have thought the roof was stripped of slates. I went to find Ruby, who (on this occasion fortunately) had not gone to bed. It seemed that everywhere I walked there was broken glass. Ruby was very frightened but unhurt, and I got a candle to investigate the damage. It was soon clear that the back of the house had received the main force of the blast, and this, of course, was natural because of the curved shape of the road. I found that all the back windows and that on the upper landing had been blown in, frames and all; the side door was blown in also, and the leaded glass of the front door was bulging but not gone; most of the conservatory glass has gone, and, with it the door smashed in two; no more ceilings are down, but there are further chunks from those already fallen; and most of the roof slates are dislodged, though fortunately still on the roof and apparently unbroken. When I had taken stock of the damage I knew well enough that nothing could be done about it till daylight and after having ascertained that the school should again be opened as a temporary rest centre and informed the warden, I went back to bed and fortunately had some six hours of sleep to fortify myself for the labours of

the day, which have been mainly the removal of debris. This time everything is covered with a thick deposit of black grime (brick dust and soot I think), which will make clearing up a big task. In this respect my study seems to be worst affected, probably because the big windows were wide open.

Before nine o'clock this morning, inquiries about our safety began to arrive, the first actually from our Thornton Heath fishmonger. And the procession has been going on all day, including in it various people with whom we have had only slight contacts, or contacts some years ago. It looks as if we are not exactly hated in this district, and one might suppose that if we had been killed the funeral might have been impressive!

When I had to go up The Crescent to do some shopping I found a scene of terrible ruin. The bomb fell on two large old semi-detached houses at the end on the opposite side. They were carried down in chaotic ruin, and their weight made the rubble pack so tight that bulldozers had to be brought to push an entry into the debris before digging could start. Six people were killed in the basement of one house, but two in the other were alive and unhurt in their Morrison shelter and were brought out after 15 hours' digging, this afternoon. The Broomfields' fine house stood next door: it has been cut in two, one half still standing, the other a cascade of ruin; the Broomfields themselves escaped death by less than a yard, for they were sheltering under the stairs which are now right on the edge of the wreckage. [The family owned the well-known local bakery and shops. One of their vans is in illustration number 16.] The houses on the other side have suffered terribly. In all a dozen have been completely demolished, and another 17 will have to be pulled down. The road, which has always been considered the most attractive in the district, is permanently disfigured for the new houses that will subsequently be built will inevitably be of different style from these 50-year old houses that remain.

The police have established a strict cordon at both ends of the road, and no one may enter without permission.

Saturday 29th July

Having seen the effectiveness of the Morrison table shelter in the wreckage of the houses in The Crescent I have decided that we should take the precaution of having one and went to the Borough Engineer's office about buying one this morning: for my salary is above the limit below which I could have one for nothing, and I shall have to pay £7 for one. It is an unwelcome but necessary expenditure. . . .

Wednesday 2nd August

All day, men employed by the Ministry of Works have been at work on repairs to the house. The enormous damage caused by flying bombs in this area has gone quite beyond the capacity of local builders to cope with it, and enormous numbers of men in the building trade have been brought from other parts of the country to keep pace with the most urgent work. Fifteen hundred of these men have been brought to Croydon alone, and since last Friday some of them have been at work in The Crescent starting at the further end where most needed doing. They have come as far as this house by today. Five or six of them were at work for the whole day on the roof, and they have put it in a sounder, more weather-worthy condition that it has been in for years. . . .

Wednesday 9th August

By dint of working really busily all day, I have regained my usual cheerfulness and serenity of mind, even though it may be only that of a fool's paradise. There was still the debris of bomb damage to clear up in my former bedroom and the attic, and this was my first job. It is noteworthy that all along the road people are still building up piles of rubble and glass and broken slates in the gutters, though the bomb fell nearly a fortnight ago; and though the debris is carted away almost daily, the heaps are continually made afresh. With the debris removed, it was possible to remove the grimy dust that had settled on everything, sifting down continually through the laths of the broken ceilings: and finally to clean down the landings and staircases.

61 Incident Post – 1944 *(below)*
The Civil Defence Service quickly set up information posts in the street after every incident. Help and advice were given and materials such as tarred roofing felt and laths could be obtained to cover glassless windows.

62 *Windsor Castle* Incident – 18th July 1944 *(above right)*
After a flying bomb fell at the junction of Brighton Road and Kingsdown Avenue, Mr W. C. Berwick Sayers, the Chief Librarian, who lived nearby, gave this description of the scene. ''A dense dirty brown smoke filled the area . . . Two houses were flattened, all roofs in sight were broken, part of the terraces of shops on both sides of Kingsdown Avenue were ragged skeletons and the thick smoke of fire was rising from the shop terrace.'' Six people were killed in the incident including a schoolboy who had been riding a bicycle. In this photograph Wardens and Civil Defence workers tend an injured woman at the scene.

63 and 64 The Crescent Incident – 27th/28th July 1944
Above (63) residents clear furniture from their severely damaged homes but at least manage to look reasonably cheerful. Below (64) a local housewife serves a welcome cup of tea to members of the Rescue Services, including one lad who looks as if he is only 15 or 16.

65 Croydon's First V2 Rocket − 1944

An explosion at Sunnybank, South Norwood, on the wet evening of Friday 20th October, marked the arrival of the first German rocket to hit Croydon.

They had been falling spasmodically elsewhere in the London area since 8th September and would continue to do so, with diminishing frequency, until 27th March 1945. Unlike the flying bombs which had mainly been launched from France, these came from the Low Countries and so Croydon was not seriously troubled. Of over 1,000 that fell in the Home Counties, Essex received 378 but Surrey only eight.

Each rocket was about 45 feet (14 metres) long, had a one-ton warhead and a range of 160 to 200 miles. They travelled too fast to be destroyed en route, and could not be heard until they exploded so no warning could be given and people rapidly came to view them fatalistically. They therefore failed as a terror weapon.

This one caused a crater 40 feet (12 metres) wide and 20 feet (six metres) deep, it killed six people and seriously injured 14 others. It made many houses uninhabitable and 59 people had to be moved to a rest centre in Suffolk Road.

It was two months before another fell in Croydon, on 29th December, and two more followed during the next four weeks. The four, all told, killed nine people and seriously injured another 14; 200 houses were damaged.

66 Home Guard Stand Down Parade − Sunday 26th November 1944

A parade of nearly 5,000 Home Guards marched past the Town Hall, as the Lord Lieutenant of Surrey, Sir Malcolm Fraser, took the salute in the presence of the Mayor and Corporation, and all the Sector Commanders. The parade is seen here in Katharine Street.

By the time the Home Guard was stood down it had achieved much and some local members had died on active service. For example, Corporal Dunn, a 55-year-old of Edridge Road, was killed at Shirley on 16th March 1944 when on anti-aircraft duty; Private Albert Giles, of Baring Road, was killed by the premature explosion of a hand grenade during throwing practice with live ammunition at Croydon Aerodrome; and Private Michael Mercer, of Godson Road, died as a result of a rifle accident. He was only 16 and need not have been in the Home Guard at all.

Victory — and the late 1940s

Thousands Parade, Singing And Dancing In The Streets,
AS CROYDON REJOICES AT END OF WORLD CONFLICT

The *Croydon Times* of Saturday 18th August 1945 carried the above headline and recorded the events of VJ (Victory over Japan) Day (the previous Wednesday). By 8.00 pm the town centre was crowded and in the Fairfield Car Park 20,000 people danced to the music of 'The Buffs'. Katharine Street was thronged to hear a speech by the King, relayed from loudspeakers at 9.00 pm. Then at 9.15 pm floodlights and a blaze of red, white and blue lamps came on and the Town Hall was bathed in light. Other buildings were also illuminated and throughout the town happy crowds lit bonfires and enjoyed parties to celebrate peace.

The remaining years of the decade were something of an anti-climax. There was a serious housing shortage, a great backlog of repairs and maintenance to most property, and shortages of many items with a continuation of rationing. Indeed it was extended to bread between July 1946 and July 1948 — a commodity which was not rationed even in the war. Croydon Council soon started a major house building programme and pre-fabricated houses appeared on bomb-sites and other vacant plots.

Then came the 1947 winter with some six weeks of snow and ice. The *Croydon Times* of 1st February 1947 claimed that Croydon was the coldest place in the South. Snow had fallen intermittently from Saturday morning until Wednesday morning, followed by a keen frost. Thousands of water pipes were frozen and stand-pipes were provided. Snow drifts at Addington and other outlying parts were four feet (1.3 metres) deep, and the pianist at a concert in the Civic Hall had, between items, to warm his hands in a bowl of hot water. There was a severe fuel shortage, street lighting was cut off and towards the end of February over 12,000 people in the town had been laid off work. More blizzards came before a thaw in mid-March, and meanwhile for fuel some people were using compressed paper briquettes made from coal dust mixed with cement, old railway sleepers and trees stolen from local woods. Offices and shops had heating for only a few hours each day and people had to work in coats and gloves.

The period also saw several transport accidents in the district including the crash of a Dakota shortly after take-off from Croydon Airport in January 1947, killing 12 people; and Croydon's worst railway accident, at Purley Oaks, in October 1947 when 32 were killed.

In March 1947 the last five Civic Restaurants closed; in 1948 the foundation stone of the new Croydon 'B' power station was laid. In the same year the Croydon Gas Company was absorbed into the nationalised gas industry, the Corporation's electricity undertaking was nationalised, and the local hospitals passed from Council control to the new National Health Service. A shortage of nurses caused the closure of some 130 beds in Croydon General and Mayday Hospitals.

By the end of 1949 war-torn Croydon was beginning to get back to a peace-time routine though rationing was to continue for several more years. Most people still used public transport and the town looked much as it had in the 1930s but the next decade would see the start of fundamental physical and social changes which would transform it.

67   VE Day Bonfire — 1945
Germany had surrendered unconditionally on 4th May, and Tuesday 8th May was declared VE (Victory in Europe) Day with a holiday on that and the following day. The country celebrated with impromptu parties and a variety of events. Streets, houses and shops were decorated. The *Croydon Times* reported that a crowd followed the Salvation Army band as it marched through the town and fire crackers exploded amidst shouts of laughter as people sang songs of both the First and Second World Wars. At times it was almost impossible to drive a car through the main streets. Thousands walked, cycled or went by bus to Addington Hills for a birds-eye view of the festivities and to see the massed waving searchlights all over London just before midnight. Thousands danced in floodlit Thornton Heath High Street, while most of the trains passing through the station hooted the 'V' signal in morse code. Hitler's effigy was burned in many places such as this where a happy crowd of adults and children cheer and sing around a bonfire in a Thornton Heath street.

32

68 Thanksgiving Service − VE Day − 8th May 1945

People thronged the main streets of the town in the sunshine of the Tuesday morning and as the day went on the crowds increased. By 3.00 pm thousands had gathered in Katharine Street to hear the Prime Minister's historic announcement of the cessation of hostilities relayed by loud-speakers around the Town Hall. Katharine Street was decorated, and at 4.00 pm a carrillon of eight bells, lent by Gillett and Johnston and erected outside the Reference Library, summoned the crowds to a short Service of Thanksgiving. Purcell's *Trumpet Voluntary* and a fanfare of trumpets began the proceedings. The Mayor, Councillor George Lewin, is seen here addressing the crowd. After a brief silence, he led the service.

For the rest of the day there was broadcast music, singing, dancing and illuminations.

69 Victory Street Party − Clyde Road, Addiscombe − 1945

During May and well into June celebration parties for children were held all over the town − in the streets, and in such venues as Community Centres, school and church halls, and workers' canteens, organised by parents, neighbours, fire watchers etc, and with contributions from local firms and traders.

In the evenings, at some of the parties, the adults took over where the children left off. Pianos were brought out on to lawns or into the streets, and dancing took place until a late hour.

Parties were again held in August and well into September to celebrate the end of the war with Japan.

70 Victory Thanksgiving Parade − Sunday 13th May 1945

This Victory Parade was part of Croydon's celebrations to mark the end of the war in Europe. The mile-long procession included representatives from all sections of the national and local war effort. It started from Fairfield Car Park and was led by the Central Band of the London Fire Service followed by units of the Royal Artillery, the Scots Guards, the Royal Electrical and Mechanical Engineers, the RAF, Civil Defence, Home Guard and Women's Auxiliaries. Some 49 units representing all the services that had contributed to Croydon's war effort were in the parade.

The procession passed through George Street, High Street, Coombe Road, Park Lane, Friends Road and High Street to assemble outside the Town Hall for the service, as seen here.

71 Removing Defences – about 1946
The immediate scare after the evacuation from Dunkirk in 1940 concerned the possibility, or probability as it was seen then, of the Germans invading this country. Aware of the methods used in the invasion of the Low Countries, not only a seaborne invasion, but also an airborne attack was expected. Consequently, urgent precautions had been taken in the summer of 1940 in the south of England, to delay or deter any would-be invaders. The larger open fields on high ground were cluttered with old vehicles and large drain pipes, and posts with wires stretched between them to hinder gliders landing. Concrete emplacements, known as pill boxes or machine gun nests, were set in strategic places to thwart tanks or other vehicles.

This picture shows the removal of concrete blocks from Purley Way after the war and gives some idea of the massive reinforcement used in their construction. A number of similar defence structures remain in some places 50 years later.

72 Prisoners-of-War – 1946
The Geneva Convention permitted the employment of prisoners-of-war in a non-military capacity and many German and Italian prisoners were used on farms and in other outdoor activities where they could work in gangs, under supervision.

They were not all repatriated immediately after the war ended and some married British girls. A few at least settled down in this country.

This photograph, which was published in the *Croydon Times* in October 1946, shows German prisoners-of-war working on a main sewer trench on the Heathfield Estate, now known as Monks Hill. This illustrates the urgent efforts then being made to resume house building after the serious loss of housing stock during the war.

There are virtually no references to prisoners-of-war in the written records of the town and there is even uncertainty as to where their camps were. The Local Studies Library would welcome further information on the subject.

**73 London Road, Thornton Heath –
Sunday 3rd November 1946**

An indication that things were beginning to
return to a semblance of normality was the
resumption of the annual Veteran Car Run to
Brighton in 1946. Harold Stillwell was on hand
to photograph an 1896 Thornycroft Steam Van
as it passed a tram in London Road outside the
State Cinema that morning.

The run was not held the following year due
to petrol shortages but it has been held
regularly since.

**74 Katharine Street – Saturday
20th April 1946**

In the 1940s the tower of Croydon Town Hall
was a notable landmark and the town's tallest
structure. This, the third town hall had been
opened 50 years previously in 1896. The
sunken Town Hall Gardens, now part of the
Queen's Gardens, were formerly the cutting
for the railway tracks leading to the Central
station, closed in 1890.

The offices on the right were the new ones
opened in 1940 by the Croydon Gas Company,
which was nationalised in 1948.

Katharine Street has long been the principal
civic street for parades of many sorts. Note the
number of cyclists present.

Arrival

Mangling

Airing

Washing

Hydro-extractor

Ironing

Departure

76 New Addington − Central Parade in 1948

In 1935 the First National Housing Trust purchased some 570 acres of Fishers Farm, intending to erect 4,400 new houses to rehouse the occupants of Croydon's slums. Charles Boot, the founder of the Trust envisaged "a village where workpeople can enjoy the beauty of the countryside". By the outbreak of war in 1939 only about 1,000 houses had been built, of which 642 were occupied. These were mostly in the roads between Lodge Lane as it then was and Gascoigne Road. Twenty-three shops had been built but only eight occupied, and four were destroyed in an air raid in 1940.

After the war when Croydon's housing need was so great, the council built 320 pre-fabricated houses and started permanent house and flat building on a large scale. The area became known as 'Little Siberia' probably because of its high, exposed and isolated situation, but perhaps also due partly to the large notice erected at the entrance to the pre-fab estate and reading rather insensitively 'Croydon Corporation Compound'.

This picture shows Central Parade in 1948; except for the off licence in the centre of the picture no further shops had been built and the landscaping and new road layout had yet to be provided.

77 Flower Show Advertisement − 1946
78 Ration Book Handbill − 1947

The Croydon Flower, Fruit and Vegetable Show at Ashburton Park became an annual feature after the war until local authority spending restrictions led to its demise. It is interesting to note that the 1946 handbill bore the slogan 'Ministry of Agriculture − Dig for Victory still' − a reminder that shortages of food and rationing continued and would do so into the 1950s. Many present-day gardening clubs and societies have their origins in wartime vegetable cultivation.

The opening ceremony was performed by the Rt Hon J. Beasley PC − Resident Minister for Australia. It was in the same year that Australia sent food parcels to help the needy in Croydon, and probably other places in the UK.

75 Public Washhouses − about 1946

Many of the older houses in Croydon were very small, had no fitted baths and had inadequate facilities for washing and drying clothes. The Corporation provided what were known as slipper baths as well as swimming baths at Scarbrook Road and at Thornton Heath. At Mitcham Road there were slipper baths and public washhouses but only the latter at Windmill Road. At the time launderettes and home washing machines were not generally available. This composite photograph illustrates the methods by which many women did their weekly wash at that time. The washhouses closed during the 1960s.

79 Sylvan Estate, Upper Norwood − about 1947

To ease the chronic housing shortage and accommodate returning service personnel and evacuees, pre-fabricated houses were erected on vacant sites. Mostly they were of one-storey and adequate for small families. In Croydon, these temporary houses were eventually replaced by permanent houses or flats, but a few still remain in some towns. The first pre-fabs to be provided in Croydon were at Haslemere Road, Thornton Heath and these were completed in 1944.

80 Oaks Farm, Shirley − 22nd February 1947

Oaks Farm was still in agricultural use in 1947 as the snow covered haystack by the trees near the centre of the photograph shows.

The 1947 winter proved to be one of the worst on record. The *Croydon Advertiser* reported that just before the end of February a surprise blizzard caused chaos after there had already been six weeks of snow and ice.

Selsdon and Addington were completely isolated next morning. Cars with snowed-up windscreens were abandoned in the streets and trams ran throughout the night to keep the tracks clear.

Corporation workmen had to use pick axes to remove ice from the pavements in some areas.

82 St George's Day Parade

Scouts line up in St John's Grove (renamed Rectory Grove in 1956) prior to entering the Parish Church for the annual St George's Day service. This photograph is thought to show the parade on Sunday 25th April 1948.

Scouts and Scouters representing some 60 troops filled the church, and the Wolf Cubs went either to St Matthew's or George Street Congregational churches.

The Vicar of Croydon, Canon Charles Tonks, conducted the service at the Parish Church, and the preacher was the Bishop of Croydon, the Very Rev Cuthbert Bardsley.

After the services, columns of marching scouts and wolf cubs, over 2,400 strong, attracted crowds to Katharine Street to watch the march past as the Mayor, Councillor Ernest Turner, took the salute from the steps of the Town Hall. The scouts were headed by the band of the Whitgift Cadets and the cubs by the pipe-band of the 5th East Surrey Boys' Brigade.

Increasing traffic led to changes in the arrangements for the parade during the 1960s and there is no longer a march through the town.

Croydon Parish Church was the largest in Surrey and before its destruction by fire in 1867 contained a splendid collection of memorials. It was rebuilt on a somewhat enlarged basis. Six archbishops of Canterbury are buried there, including Whitgift whose name is so well-known in the town. Except for those on the corners, the pinnacles above the side aisles of the church were removed in the 1950s, due to deterioration of the stonework.

COUNTY BOROUGH OF CROYDON

GIFT FOOD DISTRIBUTION

Distributions of Gift Food to aged and needy people in Croydon will be made from :—

"Electric House," Wellesley Road, Croydon, at first door past Courtyard in Dingwall Avenue, on

MONDAY	14th APRIL	
TUESDAY	15th "	
WEDNESDAY	16th "	10 a.m. to 4.30 p.m.
THURSDAY	17th "	
FRIDAY	18th "	
SATURDAY	19th "	10 a.m. to 12 noon

(A basket, or strong bag should be brought as the gifts are not in parcels.)

AN OLD AGE PENSION BOOK OR RELIEF PAY CARD MUST BE PRODUCED TO OBTAIN A GIFT, BUT MUST NOT BE SENT BY POST, OR LEFT AT "ELECTRIC HOUSE," OR THE TOWN HALL.

Applicants are advised, in their own interests, to refrain from unnecessary queueing before the opening time each day, as no advantage is gained by doing so, and experience has shown that all who call can be quickly dealt with.

There is no need to write, or call at the Town Hall or "Electric House" in connection with these gifts before the opening date for this distribution, if you already have a Pension Book or a Relief Pay Card.

TOWN HALL,
    CROYDON   H. REGAN
March, 1947   Mayor

Registered Blind Persons should apply to Bedford Hall, Bedford Park, Croydon, on the above dates and times for their Gifts.

81 Food Distribution Poster − 1947

The severe shortage of fuel during the freezing 1947 winter brought electricity cuts, low gas pressure, and coal, petrol and food shortages. The source of the food which is here being advertised is not recorded.

83 Arnhem Visitors at Trojan Factory — 1949

This photograph appeared in the *Croydon Advertiser* on 28 March 1949. It shows a group of Dutch visitors from Arnhem visiting the Trojan factory in Purley Way.

Trojan were a long-established motor vehicle manufacturer in Croydon but at this time were only making commercial vehicles such as that shown. In the 1960s they embarked on the manufacture of the 'bubble car', but the factory closed and the premises were sold in 1970.

After the war many towns developed links with places abroad. The Croydon-Arnhem link was set up in 1946. During the war a Dutch journalist, Albert Milhardo had met many British sportsmen and when peace came he was anxious to foster these friendships by establishing links between towns in Britain and the Netherlands. A tour of Britain included a visit to Croydon and because both towns had suffered extensive damage during the war, the link with Arnhem was established. There has since been a biennial sports exchange and other joint events. The Arnhem Gallery at Fairfield records the link, and contains memorabilia relating to the Dutch town.

84 Steam Train — Saturday 9th October 1948

Most of the railway lines in the area were electrified before the war but the Oxted line from South Croydon remained steam operated throughout the 1940s and 50s. Here the 3.52 pm train from Victoria to Brighton via Oxted passes Selsdon which was still a junction station with platforms for the Oxted line as well as the Woodside line. Most of the freight trains in the area were also hauled by steam engines at this time. Selsdon station closed with the Woodside line in 1983.

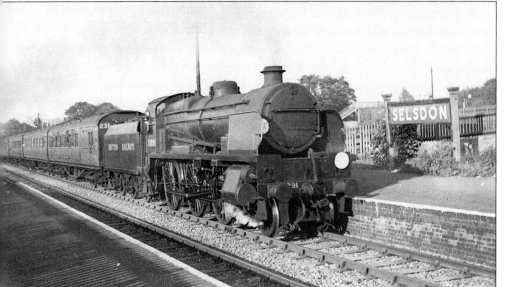

85 Shirley — Saturday 3rd April 1948
(opposite — below left)
This view down Upper Shirley Road from near the corner of Oaks Road was virtually unchanged half a century later. It shows one of the new RT type buses on route 130 and a horse-drawn milk float. The trees in the background fronted the grounds of Shirley Court, where at that time cattle could usually be seen grazing. Since 1965 it has been the site of Coloma Convent School.

86 Coombe Wood — Sunday 16th May
     1948 *(opposite — below right)*
A view of Coombe Wood in early summer soon after it was opened to the public. Coombe Wood House was built in 1898 for Arthur Lloyd. It belonged to William Cash, latterly Chairman of the Croydon Gas Company, for 37 years. After purchase by the Corporation in 1948, the house became an annexe for Croydon General Hospital, then an old people's home. It is now a restaurant — the *Château Napoleon*.

87 Norwood Lake about 1948
The lake is artificial, having been constructed at the beginning of the 19th century to provide water for the Croydon Canal which linked the town with the Thames at Deptford. The lake and surrounding land were bought by the Council in 1931. This photograph shows a party of children on a motor-boat, *The Skylark*, returning from a trip around the lake.

88 Thornton Heath Clock Tower about
     1948
A route 42 tram has just passed the station and is approaching the corner of Parchmore Road. The guard rails and Belisha beacons seem to be receiving a fresh coat of paint.

Before the introduction of central heating and smokeless zones most people relied on solid fuel to heat their homes. Many railway stations had their own goods and coal yards. There was one on both sides of Thornton Heath station. That on the east (nearer the photographer), with its road entrance on the corner served the local coal merchants, including Beatties as well as Rickett, Smith & Co, and Charringtons who had lock-up coal order offices on the station approach in Brigstock Road. Coal merchants' lorries with their sacks of coal were familiar sights on local streets.

Tesco now occupy the site of the coal yard, but at this time had a relatively small shop in Cotford Parade on the left.

89 East Croydon Station about 1948
The original station opened in 1841 and was rebuilt in 1894. The frontage then changed little until demolition and construction of the present glass and steel structure in 1991/2.

The railway bridge was widened in the 1960s and the *Railway Hotel* and buildings on the right were then demolished.

90 Park Hill – Saturday 8th May 1948
The main features of the Croydon skyline in 1948 were the Town Hall tower and the gasholders and water cooling towers of the gas and electricity works to the west of the town. The foundation stone for the new power station (Croydon 'B') was laid in 1948 just before the nationalisation of electricity.

Being so close to the centre of town, Park Hill has been a popular recreation area ever since its opening – in a snowstorm – In July 1888.

92 High Street about 1948 (*below right*)
Two trams pass the *Davis Theatre* which had a lucky escape from a direct hit by a high explosive bomb early in 1944. This came through the roof, but the ignition unit split from the explosive and the bomb failed to explode. However it penetrated to the stalls and killed or fatally injured seven people and injured 31 of the 1,500 audience. This would no doubt have been the town's worst incident had it exploded. In the same raid by a lone aircraft, a bomb fell on Allders' store and

caused severe damage there, to the roof of the Whitgift Hospital and to shop windows in North End and George Street.

In 1946 the *Davis Theatre* was the venue for the inaugural concert by the Royal Philharmonic Orchestra under Sir Thomas Beecham. The orchestra has continued its relationship with the town since.

Note that several shops on the right still had temporary windows several years after the war had ended. Their site is now occupied by the Flyover and approach roads.

91 North End about 1949
North End was as usual busy with shoppers on this bright afternoon. Many of the shops, including Allders, still used sun blinds to protect their window displays. A couple of trams, a Green Line coach, and one car appear to be the only moving vehicles. Drummond Road is on the right. Most shoppers would have arrived by bus, tram, trolleybus or train.

The 1950s

A selection of local news items for 1950 gives a flavour of the time. A grocer was fined £10 with £2.2s costs for overspending his points in obtaining rationed food (rationing ended in 1954). The minimum wage in the laundry industry was 8d an hour but it was stated that most workers actually received 1s.9d to 2s.1d hourly. Addington village school closed in January after 105 years and the trams were moved out from Thornton Heath Depot to Purley so that the former could be rebuilt as a bus garage.

The Mayor, Alderman C. H. Gibson, attended the 80th Annual meeting of the Croydon Natural History and Scientific Society where he suggested the town should have its own museum,

---

93 Surrey Street – Tuesday 30th May 1950

Looking south, this photograph was taken from the roof of Grant's department store in the High Street. On the left is the rear of the *Croydon Advertiser*'s works at 36 High Street which moved to Brighton Road in the summer of 1966.

The building with the dome on the corner of Scarbrook Hill is the *Palladium Cinema* – originally the *Orpheum*. Seating 680 people, it opened in 1914, became the *Cinema Royal* in 1925, and in 1930 the *New Palladium*. It closed and was demolished in October 1956 to make way for a six-storey block of shops and offices named Surrey House. The building next to the cinema was in the early 19th century the local jail, subsequently a shop, and was demolished in 1957. Telegraph poles were still a part of the town centre scene. The building in the right background is the Telephone Exchange.

94 The Freedom Bell – Friday 25th August 1950

This was the largest bell made by the famous local firm of Gillett and Johnston at any time after the war. It was nearly 8 feet (2.4 metres) high and weighed over 10 tons. The photograph shows it at the start of its journey from Whitehorse Road to America and thence to Berlin to mark what was called the New Crusade for Freedom.

The American Ambassador, Lewis Douglas, had been present at the casting ceremony a month previously when he had thrown a half crown and a small lapel badge bearing the slogan 'American Fight for Freedom' into the molten metal. After the casting the bell had to stand for eight days to cool.

It is not known what effect, if any, either the campaign or the bell had on the erection, and subsequent demolition of, the Berlin Wall.

something the Society had been advocating throughout its existence. A few days later a Thornton Heath woman presented the Mayor with 6,333 farthings for his 'Happiness' Fund.

On Wednesday 26th April heavy snow brought chaos. As much as 12 inches (30 centimetres) fell, causing severe damage to fruit trees and blossom. Fallen telegraph poles blocked the railway line from West Croydon to Wimbledon and several roads were obstructed by fallen trees.

On Summer Sundays large queues formed at East Croydon station for Brighton trains; the new power station was reported to be nearing completion; and a bull escaped from the Municipal slaughterhouse and ran amok in Wandle Park. Messrs Sainsbury's replanned their London Road premises at West Croydon and introduced the American-inspired 'Help Yourself' system. It was the first such branch in the country, but customers still had to obtain rationed goods at a separate sales counter.

The 1950s were years of increasing prices and wages, and improving living standards. The Festival of Britain in 1951 celebrated the 100th anniversary of the Great Exhibition of 1851 and was also intended as a boost to morale after all the post-war difficulties. Local celebrations were fairly low-key, the main contribution being the provision of the Ashburton Memorial Homes at Addiscombe.

In 1952 the sudden and unexpected death of King George VI was followed in the next year by the Coronation of Queen Elizabeth II. This was another opportunity for street parties, celebrations and decorations. It also boosted the sales of television sets as many people wanted to watch the ceremony. The great and continuing growth of this medium during the period hastened the decline in theatre and cinema patronage. The town centre grew increasingly quiet in the evenings. *The Scala*, North End, closed in 1952; followed by *The Hippodrome* in Crown Hill, *The Palladium* in Surrey Street and *The Central*, South Norwood, in 1956. *The Astoria*, South Norwood went in 1957 and then, in 1959, *The Pullman* (formerly *The Pavilion*), Thornton Heath, *The Eros* (formerly the Empire Theatre) in North End, and *The Grand* and *The Davis* theatres. There were few cafes and restaurants open in the evening but a few coffee bars sprang up as the 1950s progressed.

The year 1953 also saw the sadly notorious Craig and Bentley trial in which two youths were

convicted of shooting a policeman on premises in Tamworth Road, Bentley being subsequently hanged for the offence. There was, too, an abortive attempt by the corporation to obtain city status.

Use of the motor car and traffic congestion increased perceptively and the frequency of bus services began to fall, though many people still enjoyed a bus ride into the country, especially on Sundays.

In 1955 the Council approved a redevelopment plan for the town and in 1956 the Croydon Corporation Act was passed. It permitted the town centre redevelopment which began to take shape at the end of the decade. Many of the large Victorian houses with extensive gardens were nearing the end of their 99-year leases and were also increasingly unsuitable for modern needs. Redevelopment of these started, particularly in the Upper Norwood area, and later, in the 1960s at Park Hill. In 1959 the airport closed and Croydon's place on the world map went too. Its future importance would increasingly lie in commerce, as industry would decline in the next decades.

During the last few weeks of 1959 the local papers reported on plans to develop the whole of the Park Hill estate; problems caused by lack of support for the new *Pembroke Theatre*; and a Town Poll which followed a surprise objection to a Corporation Bill that included proposals for the Fairfield Halls. This, the first such poll of electors for 27 years, would decide whether the Bill should be presented to Parliament. A growing number of office and redevelopment proposals was reported and it was obvious the town was on the threshold of tremendous change.

Current prices included £3,500 for a modern semi-detached house with three bedrooms and two reception rooms at Coulsdon; 88 guineas for a 17-inch television set in a polished wooden cabinet; £8.17s.6d for a kitchen cabinet and 13s.6d for an 18-piece earthenware tea set at Kennards. The Corporation was advertising for junior clerical staff at £285 per annum (age 16) and £315 per annum (age 17), whilst Surrey Fire Brigade offered £10.7s.6d weekly for firemen (£10.17.6d if working in the Metropolitan area). An off peak day return ticket by train from Selhurst to London cost 3s.2d. Prices were low (except for items that were not yet being mass-produced, like television sets), but so too were wages. At least there was full employment.

95   Last Tram – Saturday 7th April 1951

Horse trams ran in Croydon from 1879 and were replaced by electric trams in 1901. Soon after London Transport was formed in 1933 a policy of replacement by trolleybuses was instituted. The local trams should all have been replaced by 1942 but the war prevented this and post-war shortages of new buses delayed their abandonment until the early 1950s.

The *Croydon Advertiser* reported that crowds of people lined the road between Purley Depot and Thornton Heath Pond to see the last tram pass. Hired by the Croydon and Purley Chambers of Commerce, in association with the Infantile Paralysis Fellowship, the trip made some £40 for IPF funds. At South End two horses were 'harnessed' to the tram by means of tapes passed from the top deck to the riders and they 'drew' it through the town to West Croydon. A line of hooting motor cars followed. In this midnight scene the tram, driven by the Mayor, Alderman Maurice Stacey, and the MP for Croydon North, Fred Harris, is turning into Brigstock Road. A large crowd surrounded it and many of the seats and other fixtures were removed as souvenirs, while several people danced on the roof.

97   Thornton Heath Pond – Saturday 21st April 1951

For centuries the pond was a well known landmark and the area still bears its name.

At holiday time, local youngsters could find their amusement fishing there, although whether they had much success is doubtful. Certainly, there were frequent comments in the local papers at this time about the condition of the pond and the amount of rubbish and debris the water contained. In 1953 the pond was filled and an ornamental garden with a small pool was provided.

In 1959 a coffee stall opposite had become a popular meeting place in the evenings for local teenagers and 'Teddy Boys' and there was one incident where a hostile gang of some 200 attacked a couple of policemen, fortunately without serious results.

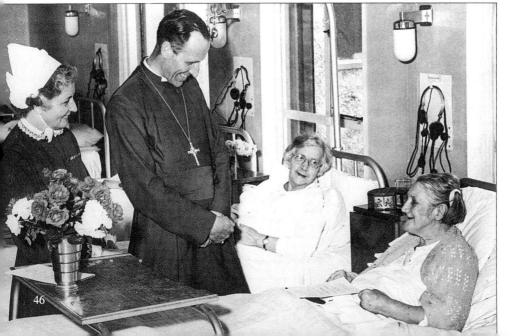

96   Queens Hospital – Tuesday 3rd July 1951

The popular Bishop of Croydon, the Very Rev Cuthbert Bardsley conducted a special service to inaugurate the Hospital's festival. He is here talking to a patient, Miss Ella Cole, while on a tour of the wards with the Matron, Miss M. A. Annand.

98 International Language Club, Addiscombe Grove

Founded in 1938 by Terence Driscoll, by 1939 the club consisted of five houses in Addiscombe Grove. In post-war Croydon there were problems with the local authority over planning permission as the club expanded to occupy some 38 houses in the Park Hill area. These housed about 500 residents, many of them students and from a variety of different races.

In the 1960s the redevelopment of the Park Hill area came with the end of the 99 year leases of many of the large houses and Terence Driscoll eventually provided purpose-built premises in the Old Kent Road, retaining just a couple of houses in Croydon.

99 Katharine Street – Friday 15th February 1952

King Georve VI died suddenly and the news broke on a stunned nation the following morning. This photograph shows the crowds gathered in Katharine Street for the two minutes' silence which was observed in his memory. The ceremony was attended by the Mayor (Alderman Leonard Aston), the Town Clerk (Ernest Taberner), members of the Council and Council officers.

100 John Canmore – May 1951

John Canmore, a veteran of the First World War, was a familiar figure in George Street from about 1930 until the 1950s. He regularly occupied a pitch outside St Matthew's Church where he is seen here at the age of 77, displaying some of his paintings.

101 New Addington Carnival – Monday 6th August 1956

As New Addington grew in the 1950s its character changed from that of garden village to local authority council estate. It developed a strong community spirit and the Carnival on August Bank Holiday Monday became a popular annual event. It drew large crowds and the current fashions are well-illustrated here. It looks to have been a cool and cloudy day, as jackets and light coats are in evidence.

The Central Parade shops were by now well established and this view makes quite a contrast with the illustration (number 76 on page 37) taken only eight years earlier.

102 Parade at Selsdon – May 1957

A British Legion Parade is marching up Addington Road. The Legion was particularly active at this time as its members included many veterans of both world wars.

Note that there was a small gap in the shopping parade near the 64 bus. This was not filled until the 1960s when branches of Sainsbury's and Woolworth's opened.

103 Waddon Mill and Factories about 1950
This aerial view shows Waddon Mill, and part of the mill pond (top left) that was filled and made into a car park in the 1960s. The River Wandle is also visible as it flows from Purley Way in the foreground to the mill. This section of the river was put in a culvert during the mid 1960s.

Waterman's Dry Cleaners is in the left foreground, adjacent is the Trojan factory and several others are alongside and behind. Commerce Way is at the top right. Many of these and other factories in the Purley Way industrial area now serve as warehouses or retail outlets.

104 Sir Winston Churchill — Monday 27th September 1954
During the war, Winston Churchill had proved a great leader and his speeches were eagerly awaited in the darkest days of the conflict.

A few days before the by-election in the Croydon North-East constituency caused by the death of Sir Herbert Williams, the sitting MP, Sir Winston broke his journey home to Chartwell to spend a few minutes at the Conservative Club at 10 South Norwood Hill. He is seen here about to enter the club, followed by the candidate, Vice-Admiral John Hughes-Hallett (who was successful) and watched by a crowd of about 200.

105 Fire at Waddon – Saturday 29th October 1955

A fire broke out early on the Saturday afternoon at the factory of Mundet Cork Products in Vicarage Road. The factory had closed for the weekend and all the staff had left. Next week the *Croydon Advertiser* reported that Croydon firemen fought for several hours to control the blaze, assisted by fireman and appliances from Purley, West Norwood and Mitcham.

Police were drafted in to control the large crowd of sightseers who had gathered to watch, attracted by the large pall of smoke smelling strongly of cork. As the firemen fought the flames, part of the roof fell in, leaving a wall flanking the railway in a dangerous condition. Train services between West Croydon and Waddon Marsh were suspended until the Sunday afternoon. The ruins continued to smoulder until Monday.

A large amount of stock was ruined by the fire but new stock was soon obtained from Lisbon as well as from other parts of Britain.

106 Civil Defence Exercise – October 1955

This took place at South Norwood Sewage Farm (now South Norwood Country Park). There was a Civil Defence training site here which included a derelict building, useful for training purposes. Although it was 10 years since the war had ended Civil Defence training was still seen as highly necessary, because of international tension.

Within the new Country Park there is a large artificial mound which has been made into a viewpoint. It was created by tipping rubble from the buildings of Croydon that had been destroyed by enemy action during the war.

**107 Last Goods Horses at East Croydon −
Saturday 9th February 1952**

The views on these two pages illustrate the
gradual disappearance of the working horse
during the 1950s. The railways had used horses
widely for shunting wagons in goods yards and
for local delivery of parcels. The *Croydon
Advertiser* reported that it was a sad day for
65-year-old Bert Andrews who left his house in
the station yard soon after daylight and made
his way to the stables to feed his five horses as
usual. At midday they were loaded into horse
boxes and Bert said goodbye to them. He had
worked at the station for 34 years and had
stayed on until the horses were replaced by
lorries.

108 Meadow Stile − November 1954
(opposite − below)

This is a short cul-de-sac situated between
Laud Street and West Street on the west side of
High Street. A short alley at the end is thought
to mark the site of the stile whence it gets its
name. The Express Dairy had premises here
from about 1930 but local distribution is now
carried out from their Kenley Depot. At the
end of the street can be seen a horse-drawn
milk cart with its shafts turned up. By 1959 the
last horse-drawn delivery had been made and
the man-operated floats which replaced the
horses were themselves later replaced by
electric battery vehicles.

**109 Horse-Drawn Coal Cart − Saturday
3rd October 1959**

This block of shops is in Lower Addiscombe
Road just west of Addiscombe station. Messrs
Harris and Bailey delivered their coal by the
traditional horse-drawn cart but this was about
to change, as was the use of coal. Croydon
gradually was made into a smokeless zone over
a five year period commencing in 1961.

**110 Eagle Hill, Upper Norwood −
Saturday 21st November 1959**

This was part of the area known as Norwood
New Town. The cottages were built in the mid
19th century for workmen engaged in building
the Crystal Palace. In the early 1960s most of
the houses were cleared away. In this view an
electric milk float has replaced the familiar
horse-drawn vehicles.

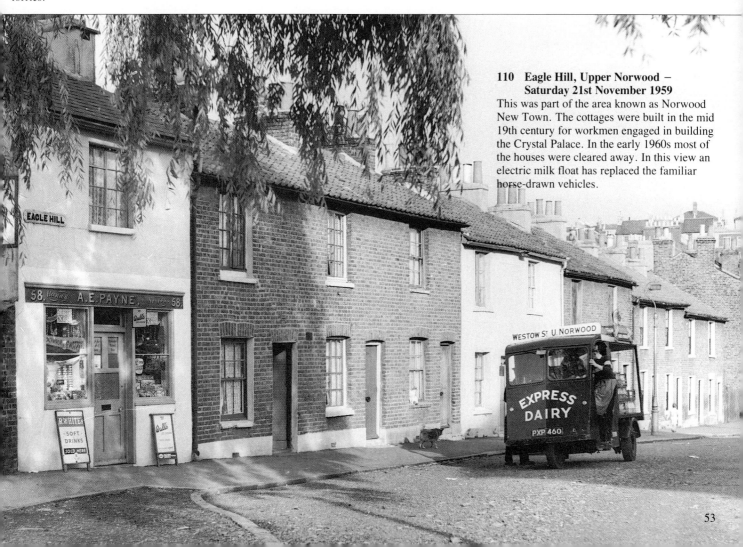

**112 Purley Cross Roads – Monday
   9th July 1956**

**113 Purley Road – Friday 5th September
   1958**

Flooding at Purley and South Croydon was a
frequent occurrence with the water running off
the downs into the Caterham and Brighton
Road valleys and converging on Purley. Here a
route 115 bus negotiates the floodwater outside
the *Jolly Farmers* in a scene quite common at
that time.

On Friday 5th September 1958 severe
thunderstorms swept southern England. At the
Classic Cinema, near the *Swan and Sugar
Loaf*, the electricity failed and for a time
patrons had to sit in darkness with water
lapping around their feet. This photograph
shows people clinging rather precariously to
the railings by the Purley waterworks with the
Railway Hotel in the background.

A major sewer relief scheme in the 1960s
brought a considerable improvement and
flooding is now rare.

111 Coulsdon North Estate − Tuesday 10th August 1954 *(above left)*

A reaper-binder towed by a tractor is seen harvesting a crop in a field behind the recently built numbers 3−10 Hillars Heath Road. The rooftops of houses in Windermere Road are visible beyond.

This farmland was developed for building purposes in the 1960s.

114 The Dutch Village, Coulsdon − August 1956 *(above)*

The Post Office Telephones Department is busy installing telephone lines at Wilhelmina Avenue, Coulsdon. The work of the builder is still in evidence although the Dutch Village, comprising Wilhelmina Avenue and The Netherlands, was laid out before the Second World War. Most new telephone lines are today laid underground.

115 Traffic at Purley − Monday 4th August 1956

Car ownership started to increase rapidly during the 1950s, as living standards improved. Already traffic congestion was reaching serious levels at times, as this photograph of traffic returning from the coast and countryside on August Bank Holiday Monday indicates. The view is north along the Brighton Road with the grounds of the waterworks behind the trees on the right. Note the boy selling newspapers to car-bound customers.

116 Tobogganing at Coulsdon — Tuesday 2nd February 1954

Happy faces greet the photographer at the Memorial Ground in Marlpit Lane, Coulsdon. The slope leading down from the tennis courts and the war memorial makes an ideal run for tobogganing. The memorial was designed by W. J. Walford and dedicated to the men of Coulsdon on 16th April 1921 following the transfer of the land from Messrs Hall & Co. to the Coulsdon and Purley Urban District Council.

117 Morris Dancers — Saturday 1st May 1954

An enthusiastic team of the East Surrey Morris Dancers provide a traditional celebration of May Day adjacent to Sanderstead Pond, and watched by a couple of amused schoolboys. The parish church of All Saints and a cedar tree make an attractive background. This small piece of common land is known locally as 'The Gruffy'.

118   Fair at Coulsdon – May 1957
This fine action shot of decorated boat swings
was taken at a fair held on Coulsdon Common
in May 1957. In the background can be seen
the Coulsdon Road at its junction with Fox
Lane. For many years until at least the 1970s
there was a permanent set of boat swings
adjacent to the tea rooms on Farthing Downs.

119 Church Road, Upper Norwood – early 1950s

There were two cinemas almost next door to each other until *The Century* closed in 1958. Originally *The Albany* and opened in 1930, it was refurbished and renamed in 1950. *The Granada* had opened as *The Rialto* in 1928 and that too was refurbished and renamed in 1950. It eventually closed in 1968. Note the 1920s style telephone box still in use and the lack of road traffic.

120 High Street, South Norwood – October 1956

This view is towards the South Norwood Hill/Portland Road crossroads, from near the Clock Tower. In 1956 many of the shops remained virtually unchanged from the 1920s although some had modernised fronts. South Norwood is one of the local shopping centres that seems to have been particularly badly affected by the development of supermarkets and retail warehouses elsewhere.

121 Croydon High Street about 1956

Looking north from near the corner of Mason's Avenue, the attractive Georgian houses on the extreme right were demolished in the 1960s to make way for Leon House and the space in front. Just beyond are the former offices and buildings of Nalder and Collyer's brewery which had closed in 1936 and was in use as a factory at this time. The dome is that of *The Grand Theatre*, opened in 1896, and closed in 1959 to be replaced by Grosvenor House.

Many of the buildings on the left, including *The Catherine Wheel* public house, have changed very little. Note that although the tram track had been removed its position was still clearly visible at this time.

122   London Road, Norbury about 1952
Hermitage Bridge over the River Graveney, where the road bends, marks the boundary between Croydon and Streatham. The tram tracks had been lifted but several of the poles which had supported the overhead wires still remained.

Before the advent of supermarkets each local community still had a number of traders such as butchers, bakers and fishmongers. Hearn and Son owned several butchers' shops in the town. *The Sussex Tavern* on the left is currently *The Brass Farthing*.

123   Wandle Park – September 1952
The park was laid out in 1890, and the lake was constructed at the same time. Initially there was sufficient water from springs to maintain the required depth, and the River Wandle was taken through the park in a separate channel so as not to foul the lake.

The original lake had one island with trees on it and early in the 20th century it was extended eastward. Another island was created, reached by rustic bridges, and boats could be hired from a small hut on the edge of this extension. By the 1930s the water table had fallen and the supply to the lake became erratic. This photograph shows that by the 1950s children could play on the dried-up lake bed, although after the great storm of 5th September 1958 the lake was again full of water for several days and people were seen bathing in it.

In 1967 a new culvert was laid across the park, the river was diverted into it, and the former river bed was filled in. At about the same time the lake was filled in and grassed over.

124   Whitehorse Road – Saturday 28th February 1959
Apart from the trolleybus and the lack of cars this view is little changed today. However the cottage on the left has gone to make way for Hogarth Crescent, part of a one-way system. The 654 trolleybus route ran from Crystal Palace to Sutton and this view was taken only three days before it was replaced by motor buses. The tower of Gillett and Johnston's bell foundry is on the left.

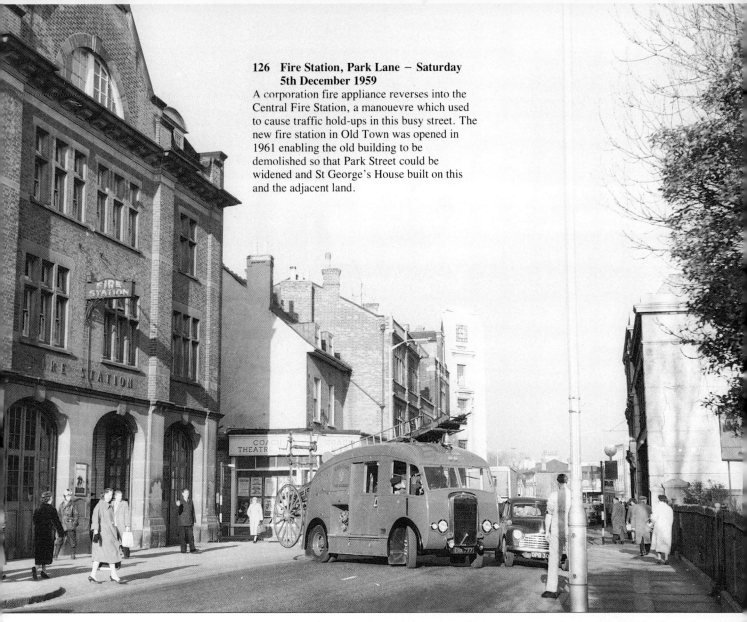

126 Fire Station, Park Lane — Saturday 5th December 1959

A corporation fire appliance reverses into the Central Fire Station, a manouevre which used to cause traffic hold-ups in this busy street. The new fire station in Old Town was opened in 1961 enabling the old building to be demolished so that Park Street could be widened and St George's House built on this and the adjacent land.

125 George Street — 1956

This photograph was taken from the building on the western corner of George Street and Park Lane, looking towards East Croydon station. On the extreme left are the Public Halls, for many years the main venue in the town for concerts and exhibitions and home of the Croydon School of Art and of the Croydon Natural History and Scientific Society.

The car is emerging from Wellesley Court Road, on the corner of which is J & T Robinson Ltd — electrical suppliers, with Ogden Smith Ltd, fishing tackle dealers, next door. The large brick building with a tower is that of John Thrift & Sons Ltd — wholesale grocers and provision merchants, who in 1960 sold out to Edward Paul & Co (Grocers) Ltd of Camberwell. The building was demolished in 1962 and those on the right went at about the same time to allow the road to be widened.

127 Fairfield and College — Wednesday 7th March 1956

Croydon Corporation bought the Fairfield site from the Southern Railway in 1934. Following a competition, plans were drawn up for a new civic centre but the war caused the postponement of the project. Eventually Croydon Technical College and the College of Art were built between 1953 and 1959. It was at the time the largest Technical College in the south. St Matthew's Church is in the background.

128 Croydon Airport about 1952

Civil activities at the airport resumed after the war in 1946. It was already clear that expansion was not possible and that London needed a larger airport. The Government decided that Heathrow should be developed as London's main airport, that Gatwick should be enlarged, and that Croydon should close.

In this early 1950s view, Croydon's 1928 control tower and terminal building form the background for two DeHavilland aircraft. On the left is a Dove, G-AKJR, of Olley Air Service Ltd, which provided services to France and the Channel Islands. On the right is a Dragon-Rapide, G-AKOB, of Air Enterprises which served the Isle of Wight and Jersey.

The airport closed on 30th September 1959.

129 Wellesley Road – Monday 16th July 1959

Looking south, the newly built Norfolk House is on the left. Construction of the underpass had not yet started. Norfolk House was the first major office development in the town. The opening speech by the Mayor, Councillor Henry Lock Kendell, was greeted by laughter and applause. He said "Like many other people, I have taken note of the speed with which this building has been erected. I will follow that example of speed by formally declaring this building open without making a speech".

The construction of Norfolk House set the scene for the massive changes which were to follow during the 1960s and 1970s.

130 *Davis Theatre* − **May 1959**

The year 1959 was an unhappy one for cinema and theatregoers in the town. The closure of local cinemas and theatres during the 1950s culminated in 1959 with the closure on 18th April of *The Grand Theatre* − a splendid Victorian building and − only a few weeks later on 23rd May of *The Davis Theatre*. Then, only a week after that *The Eros Cinema* (formerly *The Empire Theatre*) in North End closed its doors for the last time.

This evocative night view serves as an epitaph for the town's lost cinemas and theatres.

Conclusion

In many ways 1959 can be regarded as the end of an era for Croydon. The closure of the town's world famous airport and of local cinemas and theatres, together with proposals for major new commercial developments meant that the character and nature of the town was changing irrevocably and on a massive scale not seen before.

The year 1960 had been chosen for celebations of the town's Millenary − a thousand years of recorded history. It would also mark the beginning of a new era in the process of transformation from Surrey market town to city-scale commercial centre.

Some notable local events 1939 – 1959

1939 Outbreak of Second World War.
1940/1 Battle of Britain and the Blitz.
1944 Flying Bomb and V2 Rocket attacks.
Corporation purchases New Addington Estate.
1945 War ended – VE and VJ Days Celebrations.
1946 Royal Philharmonic Orchestra – inaugural concert at the *Davis Theatre*.
32 people killed in Purley Oaks rail disaster.
1948 Croydon Gas Company nationalised.
Corporation Electricity undertaking nationalised.
Croydon hospitals enter National Health Service.
1951 Last tram ran in Croydon.
1953 *Empire Theatre* converted to a cinema – *The Eros*.
Coronation celebrations.
1954 Royal School of Church Music moved to Addington Palace.
The town's last brewery (Page & Overton's) closed.
1956 Croydon Corporation Bill enabling redevelopment passed.
1959 *Grand* and *Davis* theatres, and *Eros Cinema* closed.
Pembroke Theatre opened.
Croydon Airport closed.

Sources and Selected Reading

The information in this publication has been obtained from a number of sources. For the reader wishing to study further the development of, and life in, the Croydon area during the period, the following are recommended.

Cluett, Douglas; Bogle, Joanna and Learmonth, Bob — *CROYDON AIRPORT AND THE BATTLE FOR BRITAIN 1939–1940,* London Borough of Sutton Libraries and Arts Services, 1984.
Croydon Advertiser — *COURAGEOUS CROYDON, Croydon Advertiser,* 1984.
Croydon Corporation — *OUR CROYDON,* Croydon Corporation, 1946.
Croydon Times — *CROYDON COURAGEOUS, Croydon Times,* 1946.
Eyles, Allen and Skone, Keith — *THE CINEMAS OF CROYDON,* Keytone Publications, 1989.
Flint, Peter — *RAF KENLEY,* Terence Dalton Ltd, 1985.
Longmate, Norman — *THE DOODLEBUGS,* Hutchinson, 1981.
Longmate, Norman — *HOW WE LIVED THEN,* Arrow Books (Hutchinson), 1971.
Sayers, W. C. Berwick — *CROYDON AND THE SECOND WORLD WAR,* Croydon Corporation, 1949.

The *Croydon Advertiser* and *Croydon Times* contain a great deal of useful contemporary information and may be examined at Croydon Local Studies Library.

Acknowledgements

The ILLUSTRATIONS are from the following sources and are reproduced by their kind permission. In some cases it has not been possible to trace the photographer or owner of the copyright but their work is nevertheless gratefully acknowledged.

Harold Bennett — Front cover.
Peter Byde — Number 36.
Peter Crosier — Number 11.
Croydon Advertiser *and* Croydon Times — Frontispiece, Numbers 1, 3, 4, 5, 12, 20,23, 27, 28, 32, 33, 38, 39, 43, 44, 52, 55, 57, 58, 59, 60, 62, 65, 66, 67 and 68.
Croydon Airport Society — Numbers 18 and 19.
Croydon Parks Department — Numbers 46, 47, 50 and 51.
Croydon Public Libraries — Numbers 2, 7, 9, 10, 14, 15, 17, 21, 24, 25, 29, 30, 37, 42, 45, 48, 53, 54, 61, 63, 64, 70, 71, 72, 75, 76, 77, 78, 81, 93, 94, 96, 99, 100, 101, 102, 104, 105, 106, 107, 108, 109, 110, 111, 112, 113, 114, 115, 116, 117, 118, 120, 123, 124, 125, 126, 127, 129 and back cover.
John Gent Collection — Numbers 6, 8, 12, 13, 22, 26, 31, 34, 41, 49, 56, 69, 74, 79, 80, 82, 85, 86, 87, 88, 89, 90, 91, 92, 95, 98, 119, 121, 122 and 128.
Tim Harding — Numbers 83 and 103.
Michael and Glenda Little — Number 16.
London Transport Museum — Number 35.
Pamlin Prints — Number 84.
Colin Richardson — Number 40.
Harold Stillwell — Numbers 73, 97 and 130.

The Editor and the Council of the Croydon Natural History and Scientific Society also gratefully acknowledge the help of the following in the production of this publication:

Peter Byde, Ron Brooker, Ken Carr, Ron Cox, Ted Crawforth, Katie Davis of Purley Library, Ken Edwards, Ted Frith, Ken Glazier, Tim Harding, Mike Hutchins, Brian Lancaster, Roger Packham, Colin Richardson, Lucy Rogers, Steve Roud and the staff of Croydon Local Studies Library, Tom Samson, Malcolm Starbrook of the *Croydon Advertiser*, Harold Stillwell, Dave Smith (Memories of Hendon) and Ray Wheeler.